FIVE SECONDS

FIVE SECONDS

MANGAOHE PUBLISHERS

©John van Zeist 2018

A catalogue record for this book is available from the
National Library of New Zealand.

ISBN 978-0-9864565-2-7

FVSC

FIVE SECONDS

Heaven is here and now.

Hell is here and now.

Some are trying to make this more hell.

Some are trying to make this more heaven.

People have free will, and free choice.

People are manipulated, and controlled.

People can choose to change

the world for good or for bad.

People can choose to change

the world or do nothing.

People can evolve into better beings

or revolve into the same old, and worse.

Heaven and hell

are here and now.

Heaven and hell

are only on Earth.

A moment

in Eternity.

Contents

Preface	14
Amsterdam, a journey	16
Felix Meritis	31
Brandevoort	50
L.A.P.D.	52
London, Amsterdam, Paris, and Doesburg...	54
Amsterdam, London	60
London	64
Paris	78
The Change	90
Wednesday, the 26th of March, 2008	92
The world above the parallel line	102
The hunt for the unseen	104
What does this mean?	105
Time	106
What a wonderful world	107
Conditioning of the minds	110
New Zealand's mining industry	112

Living in New Zealand	113
3D printing	116
Bragging rights, and shame duty	118
The Round Table conflict	122
A lesson from New Zealand	125
More education	128
Plato, Socrates	130
Money	132
Traditional design	134
Interest, mortgages and investments	135
Legal banking illusions	140
The global banking illusion	141
Not the Dutch mountains	142
What is it?	146
Beauty	150
Good vibrations	151
Democracy	152
Move	154
Plato, once more	155
War	158

Miami International Airport	158
Apocalcatalyst	159
The system	
Facades	160
The propaganda-marketing machine	161
Religion-chance-evolution	162
The religion of money	163
Control	164
A patsy is born	166
New Zealand's corrupt education system	168
Business	170
School control	171
New Karmaland	174
Time II	176
Beauty II	177
Choice education	179
Meeting the hovering Orb and what came from it	182
Banksters	184
Choose wisely	185
Bureaucrats	186

Free Americans, what has become of the illusion?	187
Debt problems	189
Globalisation	190
The plane! The Plane!	195
The One	196
Donald Rumsfeld	197
Party politics	
The man	
The divide	198
J.F.K.	199
One	200
Understanding	202
Global Organised Corruption	206
H. Goering	
To vote, or not to vote	208
Greed is good?	210
Objection!	213
What do you want?	214
Five seconds of Truth	217
"Inside job"	222

Note of Understanding	224
We have to transcend	225
The meaning of Life?	232
The belief industry	236
The political belief industry	240
The commercial belief industry	243
Bureaucracy	249
The core, the backbone, the heart, the essence	256
Control conflicts with "learning to let go"	258
What is it the media write about nowadays	259
But, you have to believe in something, right?	260
Become who you are	262
If I was God	266
17-09-2015	270
15-10-2015	271
Dimensions, life, or existence, after death?	272
The von Neumann probe	273
Did the orb communicate?	274
Flat Earth, round Earth?	275
Reality	276

And then there was, the word	277
The reality without this Existence	279
Growth, the failure of Humanity	
What a beautiful world this could be	280
The good, the bad, and the beautiful	
Dear world leaders	281
Raising children	284
Father and son, I	285
Father and son, II	288
The Fermi Paradox	289
Can there be life after money?	291
Towards a conclusion	294
Are we there yet?	300
Index of images	306
References	308

Preface

Four years ago I finally started to write the book that had been in my mind for many years already, but I did not start, because something was missing. Although I kept learning and understanding, it was as if I had slowly run into a huge, immensely high brick wall. Sometimes I even felt like "Le Passe-muraille"... Then after our trip back to Europe, I found the historic background, perspectives and structure that I was looking for.

It's actually funny, realising that it's been about twenty years since I wrote my thesis about design philosophy, that turned out to be about life philosophy..., that now is the basis from where this book started growing.

The structure of FVSC is based on the concept of "rondschilderen" as Rob Annema taught in his art painting classes during my years at Academy Minerva, the Netherlands. "Peindre en rond", in French comes closest to the concept, that can be applied to many different topics. In art painting it continuously uses the whole canvas, while building up the painting itself, structured and layered. One could stop at any moment and the painting would always look and feel balanced. Like life it goes in circles, but yet every time when it arrives at the same point, it has changed, it has grown, the circle has become a spiral, a helix...

John van Zeist, Aotearoa.

Amsterdam, a journey

From the tranquility of my New Zealand home to the crowded cities of Amsterdam and London after an absence of more than five years, was quite an eye opener, or, as it would turn out later, more of a can opener.

I was surprised to find that while walking along the canals of Amsterdam I saw a city that I had never seen before, although I had been in Amsterdam numerous times already when I lived in the Netherlands. Even more beautiful than I ever remembered, its liveliness, contrasts of quiet green canals with the buzzing multi-coloured Dam in front of the Palace. And a lot of building activity mixed with a lot of restorations that reminded me of the 19th century canal house we owned until a few years before we moved to New Zealand.

It was warm in Amsterdam, July 2013 turned out to be in stark contrast with the summer weeks before that. Sunny and warm, with a lot of terraced cafes buzzing with activity. First, completely open minded, ready to take it all in, we strolled towards the renowned Herengracht, with its grandeur and well-maintained mansions where offices replaced the homes of the old business families that would all enjoy the elaborate facades for still similar representational functions. And yet, with the quietness of parked cars along the canals, but with the dangers of silent bikes coming from around every corner, I very much enjoyed its organic buzz, its feeling alive, its gentle change, adapting to different times, different people, different rules, and yet still very similar to what it was like hundreds of years before. One moment surrounded by hundreds or even thousands of people, and the next moment in a quiet courtyard, with the usual statue, the grass, the brick pavement and a few green shrubs, carefully planted as to maximise every square meter to its full potential.

Yes, I think I fell in love with Amsterdam, if ever I would live in a metropolitan city again, I could imagine it being Amsterdam. I loved the colourful bricks, the planted trees, the bikes locked and linked with the bridges, the healthy-looking, long-legged and elegantly short-dressed young ladies hovering along from one street to the other, over bridges, around corners, along terraces, anytime and everywhere.

How different then was the Kalverstraat, the shopping street where most tourists would mingle with the locals, plastic throw-away shopping bags that looked the same as in any other metropole, Madame Tussauds, with the same lines of people waiting to be allowed to watch dead people, similarly boring as any other global fast food chain, or fashion chain, disconnecting local cultures for fast global profits, careless, and cold. But then, to the right, there was a porch, an opening, the entrance towards the Begijnenhof, and the Amsterdam Historic Museum.

Having lived in Brandevoort, a newly built decadent city between Helmond and Eindhoven, a suggestion of a glorious past of an old Dutch city that never existed, expressed as extended 2D facade copies, and as such built in 3D, I looked at the Begijnenhof. First its brick pavement, then the walled lawn with a statue, the row of organically grown houses, grown with each other, the small front gardens, and the one pot paint colour that connected all the houses to one bureaucratic control rule. The difference with Brandevoort, to which I'll return later, was that here the houses were all different in design, purposely as an individual reflection of the person it was built for. Different sizes, specific proportions and, especially noticeably, each had its own specially fabricated bricks, with their own shade of red-orange-brown, as was the consequence of the way bricks were made in those days. Others were plastered and painted in harmonic off white, with one exception though, the black timber house, as a reminder of how the first houses were built, with walls that were not vertical, but tilted at a slight angle, as to make the rain drop off the timber cladded walls, away from the structure and base of the house.

I had mixed feelings at the Begijnenhof: on the one hand I enjoyed being there with my son, sharing some more of the history that shaped the culture he grew up with, on the other hand the emotions it triggered with control, contrast, cold blunt decency, illusions, decadency, losses and of course gains. Because, just as the relation I had with my own father, I learned to see the good things by seeing the other side of the bad. Therefore, it was at the Begijnenhof that I remembered again why I wanted to leave the Netherlands in the first place. I ignored the somewhat oppressive feeling between the houses, the little church, the shop, the shop lady, the tourists, the tour guide, and even more tourists coming into the oasis of the Begijnenhof.

Back to the entrance porch, and to the left, we walked towards the Amsterdam historic museum, through small glass doors into a high, narrow hall, with large paintings representing the modern and old merchants and regents that gave Amsterdam its popular image. In Dutch it is called the "Schuttersgallerij", the gallery of Amsterdam's civic watch, comparable to the function of Rembrandt's "The Night Watch". It was very pleasant that, once the tour guides took their groups away with them, you could have these paintings all to yourself, walk back and forth, come up real close, but not too close because the somewhat surly guard would step up when the alarm bell would gently sound, as he did several times when the hordes came through. But nevertheless I felt it to be pleasant, our first grand confrontation with a voluptuous and familiar artistic culture, something I miss(ed) in New Zealand, dearly...

After the gallery we moved on to the actual Amsterdam Museum, formerly "Amsterdam Historic Museum", which I think is still a better name, making a more clear distinction with the other museums, but OK, it's not a real issue here so let's move on. What is far more important, is what was to come next. We all had learned about the history of our country in school, glorifying stories of heroes and battles, adventurous journeys and of distant wealth being brought home for us. For us?

Us, becoming older, we slowly got to see other sides of the story, similar to the stories we learned about other countries, especially British, or American, or Spanish, or French, or German...

Diving into the history of Amsterdam, with this colourful presentation in the Amsterdam Museum, made me aware that what I had been discussing in the last few years with numerous people on the Internet wasn't very different from the patterns of greed, corruption and violence hundreds of years ago. Merchants taking seats in strategic governmental positions, using the legal system to organise their own profit maximization. From a global perspective, what really is different now compared to then? Halliburton USA, Dick Cheney's company, made some 40 billion dollars from a corrupt war they created at the taxpayer's expense. The lesson I learned was that never in the history of mankind, a war was started for the people, but it's always the people that pay, either as taxpayers, or with their lives, either as civilians or as soldiers.

At the historical exhibition, looking at pictures, design drawings of ships, how to meticulously maximise the amount of transported slaves that could fit under the decks, reading how sick slaves were simply thrown overboard, or how the slaves would fear getting sick for getting thrown overboard, while being chained in the densely packed hull of the ship, aroused my imagination.

It was sickening, and what was even more sickening was the realisation that the same kind of cold-hearted beings that organised such enterprises are our government leaders, politicians, corporate leaders and their lobbyists today.

"Spirit of Enterprise" is what the chapter in the historical show was called. "This spirit of enterprise peaks in the Golden Age, when Amsterdam becomes a key centre for world trade and finance, but unfortunately these are also the years of slavery and exploitation. Today Amsterdam retains its reputation for dynamic commercial enterprise". In the 16th Century, the competition for power in the Netherlands was also one for religious power, which moved from Catholicism towards Protestantism, and a new group of entrepreneurs of all sorts saw new opportunities with that. My recent realisation that royalty is a strange phenomenon in a human or humane world, or in existence at all, very much based on people killing competition and declaring themselves kings or queens, was confirmed in new research by Ronald Prud'Homme. In his 2013 book "Moordenaars van Jan de Witt" (Assassins of Jan de Witt), he exposes a different version of what we learned in school, and may I say, not really unexpectedly...

The incident I'm referring to actually is one of the most famous public murders described in Dutch national history: the violent murder of the brothers de Witt by an angry crowd on August 20, 1672. Not impulsive plebs ("pedestrians" as the former New Zealand Prime Minister John Key called them), but a group of insidious conspirators were responsible for the murder of Johan and Cornelis de Witt...

During the first official regentless (Stadtholderless) period (1650-1672) "Grand Pensionary" Johan de Witt controlled the Republic adequately. But in 1672 things changed: England, France and the dioceses of Muenster and Cologne, one after the other, declared war on the Netherlands. The Republic appeared to be no powerful, well-organised match and Johan de Witt was designated a scapegoat. In July 1672 the "provinces" of Zeeland and Holland called out Prince William III of Orange to become governor. After Johan's brother Cornelis was (falsely) accused of an assassination attempt on the Prince of Orange, it was enough for the Orangists in the Hague. They decided for once and for all to deal with the brothers de Witt. The consequences are well-known, well, at least the way it was taught in our history books.

An Orange plot then? From Prud'Homme's investigation into the assassination came a surprising conclusion: behind the public lynching was a widespread conspiracy lurking on August 20,

1672. It was a conspiracy of which even William III was informed and aware. While everyone thought he was on the war front at that time, the Prince of Orange had a secret meeting with one of the conspirators in The Hague. Along with some other people from The Hague's middle and upper class, William of Orange was greatly responsible for the gruesome incident three days later. They also made convenient use of the hateful feelings that the people already had started to harbour against the "dangerous" de Witt brothers. Propaganda warfare is not of strictly modern times it seems.

On August 20, 1672, when Johan de Witt was visiting his brother Cornelis in de "Gevangenispoort", many Orangists were assembled near that prison. They dragged the two into the streets and called for the death of the brothers. The Hague militia, an armed group of vigilantes, intervened and protected the two regents. However, some members of the militia were part of the conspiracy, and they had a secret mission to accomplish. In all the commotion they surreptitiously accomplished the death sentence of Johan and Cornelis de Witt.

Thanks to new insights from his extensive archival research, Ronald Prud'Homme dares to speak about the "solution of a cold case". It is with a vivid case like this that murderous plots in our modern times come to mind. Do we trust a documented history that is (re)written for us, every time a new regime comes to power? If so, is there a lesson or two we might miss and that we actually should have been able to learn from?

Old paintings are at least as much marketing-propaganda as

they are historical documentation, since just as in modern times, the person who pays for it gets it to tell the story in the way they want it to be heard and documented. In late 19th century Europe, Napoleon de Bonaparte shook up quite some dust in aristocratic circles, resulting in great effort to get organised and get rid of that man who threatened their luxurious lifestyles. Along the way some of them saw in that chaos opportunities to put themselves in a new, even more powerful position, for themselves and for their friends who would support their very efforts as such. There are various paintings depicting men in the late 19th century with heroic grandeur, just as the paintings were an illustration of their wealth and the grand position they had in their political society. In a way they are amusing, and even if they may tell a false story, they are a documentation of that time, in every aspect. Their only lack is that they do not tell the complete story, only the version they want to be heard, and documented.

     The Netherlands, a collection of "provinces" in various variations over time, never was a monarchy, but suddenly in 1815, we had a king. It is very amusing to read from many sources how William I crowned himself king, and only in a few sources that are royalist (including that from the royal house itself) it is claimed that "he accepted the invitation to become king". As citizens from various European countries, we all learned about the great history of our various countries, vastly ignoring the deeper histories of the other countries, and even more, how they were all interconnected, and constantly leading to the same small group of people who carefully controlled an intermediate layer of bureaucratic management that formed the protective layer between, what I used to call them, the Kleptocrats and the citizens, or to be more correct, the Kleptocrats and the taxpayers.

What really has changed over the course of a few hundred years, or a few thousand years? Or just the documented history of mankind?

I'm thinking of Egypt, Sumerian Tablets, the engravings in black marble of people with a "ball" on their heads in Paris' Louvre Museum, the continuous (Orwellian) wars in and around the Middle East, my view towards the clouds over the top of the Kaimai Range...

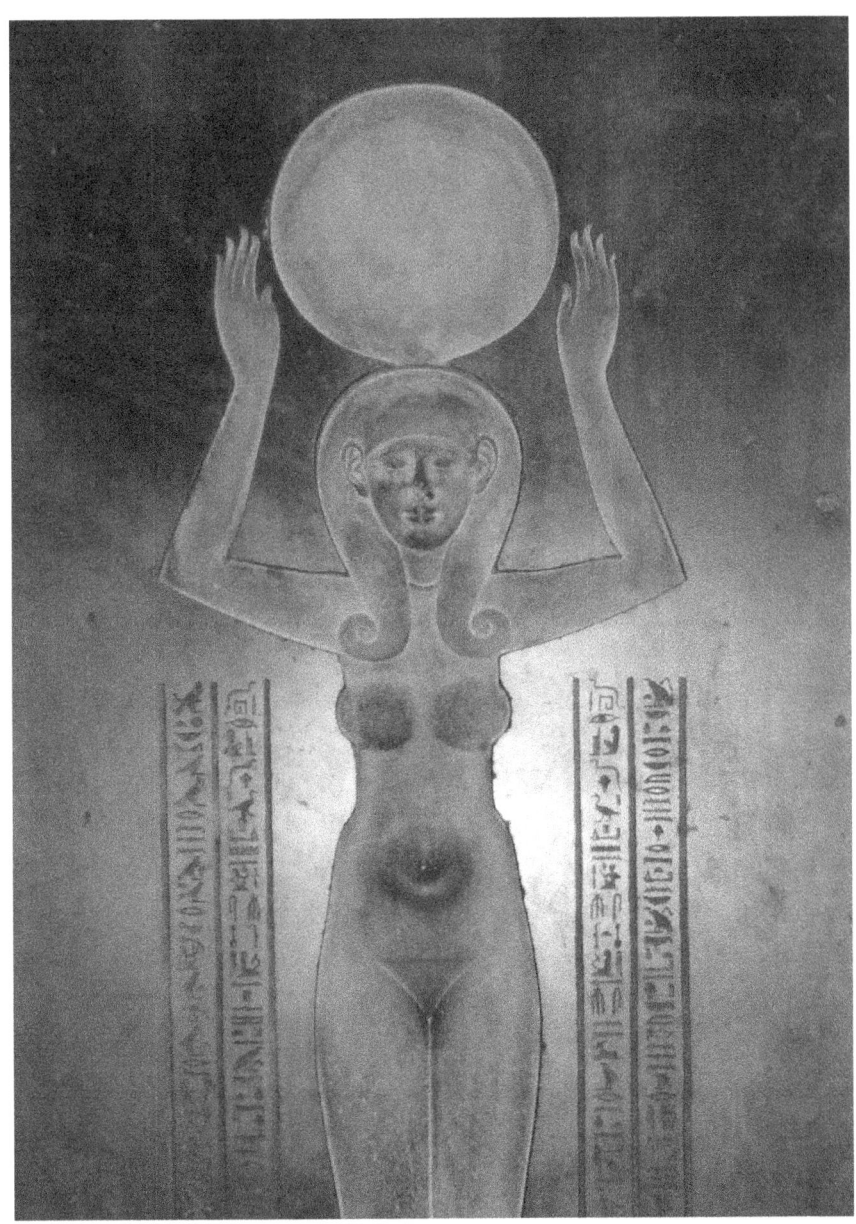

History, how it shaped our world today

After our visit to the Amsterdam Historic Museum a strange feeling came to me that could have been the opening in my mind I had been waiting for. The connection between here and now, there and then, its logic, its illogic, its continuation, repetition and change. The gateway through the wall, or was it just a gate through a wall?

What exactly was the awareness that was coming from this? The mixture of surprisingly pleasantly experiencing Amsterdam the way I never did before, and the stab in the neck from seeing how deeply rooted the current global bureaucratic system is in the way our current societies are structurally corruptible and corrupt. The deja-vu that also is a new awareness, like a new dimension and a new perspective, a circle, a loop towards a new level, a spiral, a new bird's eye view. New, that's what it is, and yet so very familiar. Some people say all of this is not real, it's an illusion, a projection of the mind, a hologram. I used to think, nonsense, how would the complexity, the amount of details, structures, layers, dimensions, all that I'm experiencing be any kind of projection?

But then another awareness occurred; the awareness that time never had a beginning. And if time never had a beginning, then existence also never had a beginning.

"Time never had a beginning, we're fooled with illusions and false beginnings, making us think there have only been a few people before us. Now, if time never had a beginning, then existence also never had a beginning. That means endless creatures before us! Endless experiences before us. Endless realities already were before us. If existence never had a beginning, then anything is possible, even what we now think is impossible", is what I wrote on December 21, 2012.

So, if time never had a beginning, and anything is possible, even what we now think is impossible, then why could all of this not be a projection of the mind? And what is a mind anyway? Am I a mind that is projecting all of this into existence? Then what is existence?

Felix Meritis

Felix Meritis, Keizersgracht 324, "Happiness through Merit". While strolling along the Keizersgracht, the Felix Meritis building stood out with its huge columns, in grey and off-white, and a sign inviting us for a visit. I enjoyed the bare timber on the inside, suggesting a proper restoration was going on, or maybe just a view back in time, with naked timber without the layers of paint covering it up in ever more distant thickness. It was actually what I hoped to find when I was restoring our mansion on the canal in Groningen, but that was immensely damaged by "the (ignorant) fashion of the day" in the 1970s. When I painstakingly restored the front doors, seeing every chisel stroke executed by someone a few hundred years before me, carefully removing old layers of paint, I felt great respect for the effort and time someone put into those doors, I felt great respect for that piece of timber and felt the responsibility of preserving it for future generations, to enjoy and to learn from.

So, seeing all this detail, in the original timber doors, frames, cornices, all so very much alive, connecting the here and now in such a clear naked moment, was sheer bliss. I imagined the 18th century with this society housed in this very same building, putting effort in better understanding and exploring science and art. It reminded me of what I had just written as a submission for a "new" New Zealand constitution. Considering proper education, I came up with S.N.A.P., meaning Science, Nature, Art, Philosophy.

Proper education teaches how and why to become more

human, more about who we are. It teaches us to work to live, instead of to live to work.

Education has been systemically hollowed out to create the workforce/wage slaves that the Kleptocrats, the Corporate Controllers, the illusions of Royalty, want us to be, to just do the jobs that they need us to do. History teaches us that it repeats when people do not learn, even worse: a downward spiral. Properly educated people would be naturally balanced, they would understand what (their) lives are about, and enjoy, respect that of others. Enjoy diversity, but also see and understand the pure injustice of inequality.

2400 years ago Plato described in his book "the Republic" the structures and consequences of bad government. If we would have learned, would we have let it come this far? The state of control, financial manipulations, the militarisation of police in all corrupted countries, the corruptible bureaucratic law system itself, would we have let it come this far?

S.N.A.P., as I proposed in my 2013 submission for a new New Zealand constitution, should be universal. Science, plus Nature, plus Arts, plus Philosophy. And the sustaining subjects for ALL 4 columns: Mathematics, History, Sports and Language. And not the corrupt "Panem et Circenses", "Divide et Impera"-based education system we now have dominating in the Anglo-American world. We are not work slaves, we are humans, when we enjoy our lives we'd even enjoy our work and produce more for the entire humanity, to grow, become better, become more complete.

We're not here to work, we're here to live, enjoy and learn, for ourselves, and for humanity. That is why we should be working to live, instead of living to work. It is time to end that cruel game, it is time to get rid of that cancerous monster that is infiltrating, manipulating and controlling our lives, ever more corruptly. It's time to heal, and create the Heaven on Earth that this place could be, for us, for our children, for our future. A healthy future.

Part of the submission for a new Constitution for New Zealand I wrote in 2013:

"Education.

The current educational system is aimed at preparing the 'pedestrians' for doing a job that benefits a distant elite. We now live to work, instead of working to live. The system is not aimed at making better persons, better humans, but better workers. While 50 years ago dreams were made of short working weeks and a lot of quality leisure time, those dreams have been taken away because somewhere along the way the goals of our societies had been changed. Suddenly we were held captive in a constant state of fear and control. Wars have become a state of mind where there is little room for expression and creativity, or learning what life is really about.

Science, Nature, Art and Philosophy (S.N.A.P.) should together form the 4 pillars on which healthy education could build, while Physical Education and History should be sustaining subjects for all 4. The reflection and understanding of these subjects will form a better society, more caring about what really matters, and not just money and materialistic possessions. With a society that has better education and understanding, comes a democratic system that is more balanced and is better capable and motivated of making responsible decisions.

Time never had a beginning, therefore Existence also never had a beginning. Once you understand that you'll see that anything is possible, even what we now think, in our limited dimensions, is impossible. The restrictions that organised religions and manipulative politicians have put on the spiritual and mental development of our society, on our humans, should be carefully discussed, and limitless structural healthy growth guaranteed by a healthy Constitution."

But, what we actually came for, at Felix Meritis, was the view from the roof. A 360-degree view over the lower roofs in central Amsterdam. And while this view used to be a platform for 18th century astronomers, it now had become a new perspective to watch Amsterdam, actually more than one new perspective. You can watch what is on the other sides of the canal facades, or watch these same facades from a higher perspective, the streets, the street life, or actually see how a densely populated area gets to grow into one large building structure, where old and new become an organic mass, more or less determined by more or less regulations in different times, and by different people... Again, just like the different generations that left their traces in the old mansion in Groningen, but then on a different scale. Here in Amsterdam it sometimes felt awkward, as if I was spying on someone's life, which however was triggered by the current changes in spying laws around the world. I was looking for different angles, different points of view, a different look than the usual one from street view level, surprises. While some of it wasn't surprising at all, some of it was. I think I mostly was surprised by the lack of continuation of effort that most people put in the looks of their facades, as if they couldn't care less, as long as it serves its basic function: space, living space. Exceptions to the rule? Hardly, maybe the ones that had a ground level garden and put a predictable, fashionable, design effort in every square meter; the long, narrow pond ("the water feature") with stone tiles along the sides and the carefully manicured grass filling the rest of the limited space, suggesting that long ago "Nature Was Here"...

FIVE SECONDS

On our way down from the "towering" observation platform, we were treated on a few spectacular interior views of the old building, where history had manifested itself in so many directions. From the original Renaissance group that were "Happy through Merit" for exactly 100 years, to the printing house, the communist party, the theatre under Ramses Shaffy's leadership, it was and still is a building that is so very much alive. Alive with history, alive with all the struggles, emotion, drama, and all left their traces in and on the building as to where and how it is now.

For my 1997 thesis "O.A.C.C.I.S."* (Observe, Analyse, Communicate, Concentrate, Integrate, Syntegrate), a journey into design philosophy that turned out to be life philosophy, that actually is the foundation for this book, I wrote a small chapter about old buildings, while thinking about becoming an architect, designer of all sorts, imagining how I would change the world with my architectural views and visions. Changing it for the good of mankind, and enjoying that journey. Oh, how that journey got messed up...

* the actual name of my thesis was OACIS, but because of the then popular band Oasis I didn't want to make it seem as if I had chosen that name for its similarity with Oasis, so I added another "C", for "Concentrate", as part of the design process...

"Traditions and Monuments.

As the old cock crows, so crow the young. Continuation of old habits and traditions often results in a style of building that leaves no room for new developments which come with growing knowledge and understanding. Traditional building methods show that in the mind of a builder or client no acceptation has taken place of new knowledge and insight. Standstill in building therefore is standstill in thinking. Here we have no opportunities for syntegration: a scary thought.

So, what then should we do with old buildings, monuments? Flatten them?

Old buildings show us, how long ago, people thought about building, it is a reflection of time, of thought, of people. Our history, our continuous development, as human beings, as individuals, is readable like a book in the numerous living forms that developed over the years, and now show us how we've grown from one stage to the next. Monuments are a lesson to learn from, to see change, "progress", where am I coming from? I receive a lot of enjoyment from imagining people in different times and how that reflects on how they lived. Was the expression of a house the cause or the effect of a certain way of living?

When did people decide to build differently? What made people decide to live differently?

When will people decide to build differently?"

Ah well, we were on our way down in the Felix Meritis building, "Happy through Merit". I noticed the grand piano in the dismantled theatre, the integrated bookcases, the joyful high ceilings. Frank Lloyd Wright said about the height of ceilings: "Anything above six foot tall is just a waste of material", and of course I used to believe him. But then I realised the different heights in the ceilings of my first tiny house in the woods, then the mansion along the canal, and how I noticed that this space around my head seemed to give me "room for thought". And in this theatre, again I had that feeling of space, as if thoughts could actually breathe. A deep sigh would connect me with the entire room. With great respect I tried to keep a distance to Ramses Shaffy's presence in that room, while at the same time enjoying it. "Zing, vecht, huil, bid, lach, werk en bewonder"...

I'm happy with everything that Amsterdam had given us in that one week, the good and the bad, the happy and the sad, the beauty and ugliness of truth. Maybe because living far away, for some five years now, maybe having become aware of the cultural, societal differences between Dutch, German, Scandinavian and French on the one hand; and British, especially colonial British, American and Kiwi on the other hand; maybe just getting older and wiser, maybe the joy of intense days of walking along the canals, in and out courtyards, houses, museums, restaurants; sharing the warmth of Amsterdam with my son, now at an age where things start to make more sense, and sometimes less, well, nevertheless, I noticed that I had fallen in love with Amsterdam...

FIVE SECONDS

When we left Amsterdam, we went south to have a quick look in the last village where we lived before leaving for New Zealand: Brandevoort, a modern, decadent illusion of an old city, created with the 2D facades of mainly old merchant houses, complete with the water features, canals and pond, though all very small, but with the price tag that comes along with decadence. I remember the bureaucracy, the corruption. It was the last straw that made us leave the Netherlands. But, it must be said, after living in New Zealand for some years now, the bureaucracy and corruption are even worse in New Zealand, but it is so much more hidden in the British colonial culture, or even legal structure, that for an outsider is almost impossible to see. I think even most New Zealanders do not see it, because they grew up with it. So, does that make Brandevoort less bad now then it was? I guess not, but I surely did enjoy seeing it again.

FIVE SECONDS

L.A.

P.D.

London, Amsterdam, Paris, and Doesburg...

A large part of my youth I spent in Doesburg, an old village with its old core built around a huge, now restored, church. That was how it was done in those days, the political power of organised religions has historically been the organising power of many a large building, and many a large piece of art, and many a large collection of land and other forms of wealth. The size of that church had always struck me as odd for the small size of the village, especially in the old times. Happily the core, the heart of this village is still standing in good shape, but the danger of greedy real estate developers is always scratching on the borders for new opportunities, no matter the consequences for the long term. I did like the new developments though, on the side of the river, a contrasting cluster of modern apartments on a peninsula, with a narrow line of water marking the divide and the connection of old, with the new.

In the old central district I was surprised to see that the old Haanappel garage had disappeared and a Brandevoort-style house had replaced it. The evolutionary growth of the old village had been replaced by a cosmetic illusion, carefully fitting in the traditionalist fashion of the day. The glorification of the illusion of the good old days. Why are we so fond of creating a fake historic image, of recreating history? What is the justification of creating false images? Surely it can not just be money, or profit? Or is it?

We strolled along the organically formed bystreets, narrowing down, widening up, coming to a meeting point of streets, small or large, the typical noise of rattling tires on cobblestones of the very few cars on that hot summer's day...

When I was a kid we lived in a stylish brick bungalow on the banks of the old river, with the bird sanctuary on the other side. As a small boy I would take the canoe and explore the island, from a safe distance on the water. And only together with friends we would explore on the island, for there could be danger... I would also swim in the river, scaring the hell out of a few adults passing by, I thought that was cool. I loved the little old river, meandering along, protecting the sanctuary island as a natural border, and a living organic entity to engage with, respectful, and caring. And sometimes the meeting place with swans that would attack you when you came too close to their nests, or the terrible smell coming from their nest, even from a relatively large distance, when an egg had not developed and started to decay...

We had the first colour TV of the village, I think it was about 1968; my father was proud of beating "the competition", and I would take friends from school to watch the TV from outside through the window, just showing the test screen, in colour! There were only a few TV shows in colour on the two TV networks, that would only broadcast in the evening.

And on that hot summer's day we went to buy a few ice creams. I looked at the lady behind the counter and realised she must have been about my age. She felt familiar. She had a pleasant presence and I was tempted to ask who she was, to investigate if we'd known each other, if we had been to school together. But then I realised that in all those years many people would have come to live in the village, and many would have gone away. She could have been anyone, and we would be gone again in a day, so I left it as it was, not disturbing their lives, not disturbing our lives, yet enjoying the moment with my family...

Hmmm, ice cream under the big shady tree.

FIVE SECONDS

As a child, I thought royalty was a fairy tale that really existed, I thought they must be beautiful people, with great minds, great hearts; wonderful people, living in a wonderful world that they deserved to live in, because they were beautiful. I thought public servants were public servants, I thought my future would be in a job I would enjoy, with a lot of leisure time, with a lot of leisure toys to enjoy and learn with. I remember the advertisements with healthy, happy people, in hovering cars, in sunny weather, with futuristic buildings, or in voluptuous Nature.

And I thought that politicians in our governments must be the brightest, best informed, best educated, most caring and involved people to be selected for such a job. People to look up to, just, role models of the highest moral standards.

Amsterdam, London...

What is any so-called royalty but a scam, based on an illusion that grew into its current form as it learned to carefully pull the strings, together with other kleptocrats; the royal illusion?

In this endless Universe, there is this tiny planet with humans where a few managed to create an illusion of superiority that legally justifies them in their corrupt(ed) law systems to steal from the entire planet, to constantly rob the entire humanity from healthy, peaceful lives, prosperity and progress.

Surrounded by corrupt profiteers in both commercial and government positions, they have created a sub-layer of servants that do the jobs of creating and sustaining their corrupt system.

We could have Heaven on Earth.

What is royalty but blind for its selfish decadence?

While on the one hand royalty is an illusion, what really is royal about any royalty in this day and age?

I think I've never seen it so clearly as now, how royalty is based on nothing, but a complete illusion, kept alive with the help of people who benefit from that illusion; a closed circle of corrupt bureaucrats and corrupt business people. When I look at my own family history, and my family history comes from several branches of knights, then the way I think, live and feel is way more "royal" then any royalty on this planet. What is royal about any of the royalty we have? Their decadent life styles? Their arrogance? Their well-hidden corruption? Their evil manipulations? Their large portfolios with secret shares in energy, mining, financial businesses or war businesses? Their interests in financial terrorism? Their claims of ownership of this tiny planet in this limitless Universe?

What is royalty but a decadent, corrupt illusion that creates selfish, evil, cold-hearted, arrogant actors as role models for the brainwashed masses? "Panem et Circenses", another spectacle to amuse the pedestrians. Are we amused yet?

Bread and Spectacles, spectacles of all sorts: TV actors, TV heroes, TV royalty (the so called "rich and famous"), disasters (natural, community, wars), to keep the masses (the taxpayers) amused, doped, busy, or even in so much fear, that they will not engage in critical thinking, educate themselves, become informed, balanced, mature citizens that do not need guidance from a self serving upper class (the kleptocrats), with the help of bought media that carefully select what information the masses will get, in what form, how long, at what moment and by who. The "Bread" as we all know by now, coming from multi-nationals, in fast food or pret-a-manger packages, chemically balanced with ingredients that create an addicted flock of "craving" carnivorous sheeple, that will have their mouths watering at every new TV ad suggesting a new flavour of the same old bite-sized snacks and sparkling drinks.

City life with its continuously glimmering advertisements, a kind of continuous pressure on the mind to keep living to the norm of fashion, of what marketing (the commercial branch of propaganda) tells us we should buy, as to fit in a normal, consumerist society. Consuming as amusement. "What are you going to do this afternoon?", "Oh, I go shopping".

With dubious amusement I watch those people with shopping bags that have the names of shops, brands, logos, printed on them largely, just to show you've been in that particular shop, or have bought that particular brand? Some of them even seem to look as if they've been reused for the illusion?

Imagine a world without brands, or even a world without money. No cash money, no checks, no electronic money.

I'm sure I'm driving a few people nuts with just the thought of it! If not for particular brands, what would the purpose of their lives be? If not for money, materialistic possessions, how could you prove you're "worth" more than others? Is that what we want? Is that what we need?

London

After a week in Amsterdam and another week travelling through the rest of the Netherlands we were ready for our trip to London. I was prejudiced with what I expected to find, and was quite aware of it. Impressed with the amount of bureaucracy and its inherent corruption in New Zealand, there was no doubt for me that the basis for that must lay in the heart of the British Empire: London.

Nevertheless I also was determined to have a great time, a great experience, especially for my son, who had never been to London before.

The London-Heathrow Express was a joy. As with all trains, anywhere in the world, coming into metropoles by train, they always go through the ugly, industrial, impoverished regions first, before taking you to the humming centre of where you were destined to go. It's like a no man's land, a border between the world where we live and a densely populated fashionable place that we all focus on, where we all need to be, because everybody does, because it is where the money is, the glitter, the latest craze, the special festivals, where the kings and queens (of all sorts) go to make their important announcements, where we go to listen, see, take in, the buzz, the marketing, the entertainment, the propaganda, the illusions..., and the realities. Of real people, their struggles, their energies, their arts, their passions, and lack thereof... A concentration of human lives, their structures in buildings and organisations, bureaucracies during daytime, and entertainments during nighttime. And in the meantime we keep eating and drinking the food that is prepared for us in restaurants of all sorts, anything from fast food to high cuisine. "Panem et Circenses" still is hiding the "Divide et Impera", history repeats when people do not learn.

When we came in our hotel we first had a room on the top floor, but with a view directly into the offices of bureaucrats that I had desperately been trying to avoid. So a little later we had a room one floor lower (not that you'd notice apart from the fact that it showed slight traces of having been occupied more often), but at least with a view...

"Paddington Station". Because it played a specific role in the numerous adventures of "Struikelpontje", the main character in one of my son's early childhood adventurous stories, I felt this was the perfect opportunity to finally go see it, and actually be there. Entering Paddington Station through "Smoker's lane" already was an adventure, non-smokers to the left and smokers to the right, and the occasional rebel on the wrong side, which as it quite often turns out, actually was the right side, hmm...

Onto the subway trains to... Trafalgar Square. We returned to daylight at Piccadilly Circus, that seemed to have become Piccadilly Semi-square, swarming with backpackers in colour-coordinated nylon backpacks with uniform logos, many of them stating "language education" of some kind. Why then were they teaching Spanish in the middle of London?

Colourful advertisements moving around bent corners were competing with the charms of a distant past, a lonely archer whose arrow still is captured in a moment of thrust, waiting for someone right in front of him to release some of humankind's dearest wishes, to come true… But the moment was ruined by some shepherd calling out to his flock some informative soup of the day, which I imagine to be the local auditive horror for any security person, assigned to the specific place and time on a schedule of this week. It is as if the contrasts of beauty and ugliness have never been competing harder than here, or is it that finally my threshold of tolerance has been reached?

Trafalgar Square, more contrasts? The Blue Cock-a-doodle-doo against a backdrop of traditional masonry, the masses in the square, unaware of the protesters marching just beyond their visual scope, the different colours of different people from different cultures. Beauty and ugliness are hitting home, and I'm fighting it, it's making me angry, and I do not want any of it. It's making me want to shout to the boringly amused zombies: "Wake up! Don't you see the realities around you?". But then I see my son, my wife, and am taken back to my responsibilities as a family father, husband, and… carry on.

However, it was then that it started to appear that this might be the last opening of awareness I needed to start writing the book that had already been forming in my head for more than ten years…

With continued time and more visual input it started to feel like a release, like a key, as if I both found the huge gateway and the key to get through the immense wall I had felt in my head. A wall which this enormous load of information had been piling against, and now there was a release. I could let go, enjoy more of the scenery, while taking it in more freely, from every angle.

London, a modern day voluntary concentration camp, filled with decent control cameras, where we all seem to think we're free to go or leave... Spy cameras, control cameras, legalised intrusions in our lives, for the control rooms of our lives, where the reality of the Matrix enters our dimensions. Fear has become a marketing instrument. Marketing has become propaganda. The illusions of reality have become our truths. George Orwell, Aldous Huxley, Joseph Goebbels and Edward Bernays became one...

Who is watching the watchers? Who is watching the watchers that watch the watchers? Are we there yet?

FIVE SECONDS

FIVE SECONDS

FIVE SECONDS

FIVE SECONDS

PRIVATE PROPERTY

The Public are not
Permitted to use these
Grounds or Roadways

NO TRESPASSING

Paternoster Square is private land. Any general licence to the public to enter or cross this land is revoked forthwith. There is no implied or express permission to enter the premises or any part without consent.

Any such entry will constitute a trespass. Limited consent is hereby given, but can be revoked at any time, for entry on to the accessible parts of the square, solely for access to the offices, retail units and leisure premises for genuine building, retail and leisure purposes. Visitors must at all times comply with the directions given by our security personnel.

Paris

What about Paris? Paris was our last holiday destination before we emigrated to New Zealand. The elegance of Paris, or even the French in general, is often copied and hardly ever understood. It's ten years ago now. The difference between Paris and London, is a difference in scale; the human scale versus the financial, bureaucratic scale.

The height of the buildings in the centre of Paris, their ornamentation, their connection to the past, with its people. It reflects a human scale, a humane scale, an intrinsic connection with its people, despite its grandeur. In London I see the distant high-rises of a financial bureaucratic elite, not with the people, but defensive, aggressive, against the people. Showing off their cold-hearted financial wealth, not caring about humane wealth.

Does this mean there is no cold-hearted greed in Paris? Of course there is, but the basic attitude, the general meaning of a building is significantly different. The word "bullying" applies; it was in New Zealand, the British colony, that I first learned about that word. There are lessons to be learned here, if one dares to see. And surely not the last lesson to learn is the meaning of "royalty", kings and queens, cold-hearted decadence, then and now.

FIVE SECONDS

FIVE SECONDS

FIVE SECONDS

FIVE SECONDS

ZEISTGEIST

Fragen
ohne Ende.
Es scheint mir
die Welt dreht
sich.
Der Kern kommt
aber näher.
Füllt mein Herz
bis über alle Grenzen.
Hoffnungslos
sich zu stellen.
Die Welt
ist mehr.

1997, Oakland, California.

FIVE SECONDS

The Change

Wednesday, the 26th of March, 2008

The day started like any other day, like any other day in my life, since Tuesday, the 26th of February, 2008.

Flashback. On that Tuesday, the 26th of February, we went looking for a plot of land in the countryside to buy and build a house on. This particular piece of land was about 40 kilometres from where we lived at that moment. As we'd been looking at several pieces of land already, and would like to compare them from the comfort and ease of my large computer screen, I always took pictures, because experiencing the land live was one thing, but taking your time to study what you've seen is quite a different thing. In pictures, I learned, you see things that you did not notice when you were there. Normally that would mean seeing and judging aspects for practical reasons, comparing details of one object with another etc., but this time, as it turned out, the pictures showed something else. And as an experienced photographer I noticed it did not make sense.

There was a bright white spot in some of the pictures, that seemed to move a little bit, altered its appearance, and was too big to be a faulty pixel. It actually had a shape that suggested to me it was "a thing". A thing that hovered over the hill in the pictures, that stayed in one spot at first, moved, disappeared, moved back to the first spot, and then seemed to have changed its appearance from a opaque white ball into a metallic ball.

It did not make sense. However, it did fit with the two pictures I made a few weeks earlier from the deck of our house, straight up in the sky, where a round white object appeared, and moved to the middle, the centre of the picture. I didn't think anything of it then, it just did not make sense. But with the pictures from "the hovering orb" it started to make sense, in a way.

We used to have military airplanes flying straight over our house regularly, as the landing strip of Hamilton Airport pointed straight towards our house. When a large C-130 Hercules comes over for the 3rd, 4th, 5th practice run, the spectacle becomes a bit annoying, a bit scary even, but in a way they also were fascinating. I often took pictures of them and with increasing regularity started to see white balls under them, in the pictures. I still do not know what they were, if they were orbs (the size would correspond to about the size of a basketball), or if they were seedpods that, out of focus, between me and the airplane, would form a visual illusion of a ball. I still do not know, but what it did do was direct me towards a phenomenon that was called a "foo fighter".

During World War 2 pilots on either side of battle would see similar hovering balls of light, and thought they would be a highly sophisticated new weapon from the enemy. The American "Project Blue Book" refers to many such incidents, but leaves no reliable conclusions, as the "foo fighters" have no claim to fame, or as to exist at all.

Time passed by, I kept researching and learning about the phenomenon, and then Wednesday, the 26th of March 2008 came.

FIVE SECONDS

    It was a gentle day, cloudy, but light. I enjoyed living in a gully, as it felt deeper into Nature, and often would take my binoculars to look at the birds flying through the gully, especially the hawks. I don't remember what I was looking for in the sky, when suddenly, moving from left to right, from West to East, the view was filled with a transparent ball that had a gently glowing light structure in it. The shapes immediately reminded me of an apple core. I wanted to look up from my binoculars to see what was there, but was afraid I could lose the sight if I did. So I focused, I registered the information, without interpreting it, there was no time for it, I thought I could do that later. Split-second decisions. I looked and studied to take in as much information as possible, the shape, the size, the structure, its brightness, its angle, its logic, its appearance, how the details related to each other, and then it moved behind trees, and I looked up, walked a bit back and forth on the deck to see if I could get a glimpse around some trees, but no. It was gone. I think I stayed out on the deck for the entire rest of the afternoon, to see if it would come back. Maybe it did, but I didn't see it.

For a moment I thought "OMG, what happened here, have I gone crazy?", and then the only thing I could do was try to come to grips with it, let it sink in, "How am I going to tell my wife, what will she think of it?", after all she is a psychiatrist, and "How am I going to tell my son?", very bright, but only 9 years old...

That evening I decided to make a painting of it, so that I would not lose any detailed information, proportions and colours. As I was observing from a slight angle, from slightly under, the dark shady spot at the bottom, was confirming a shape that I later learned to be called a torus.

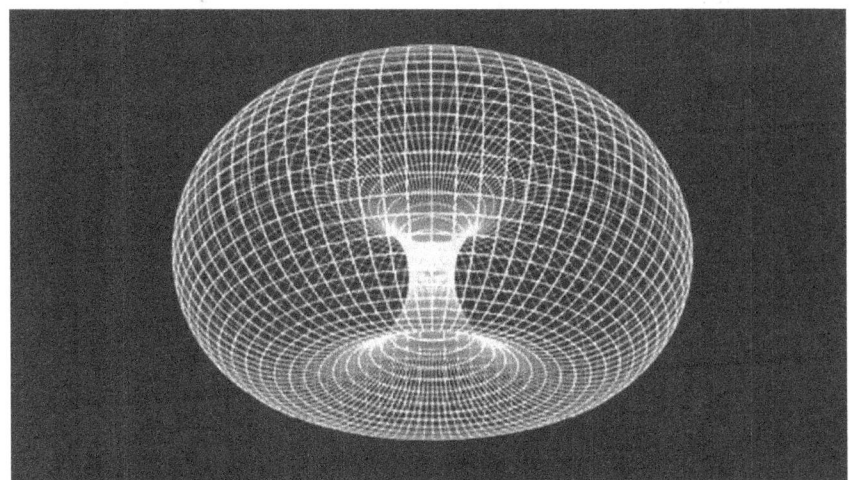

FIVE SECONDS

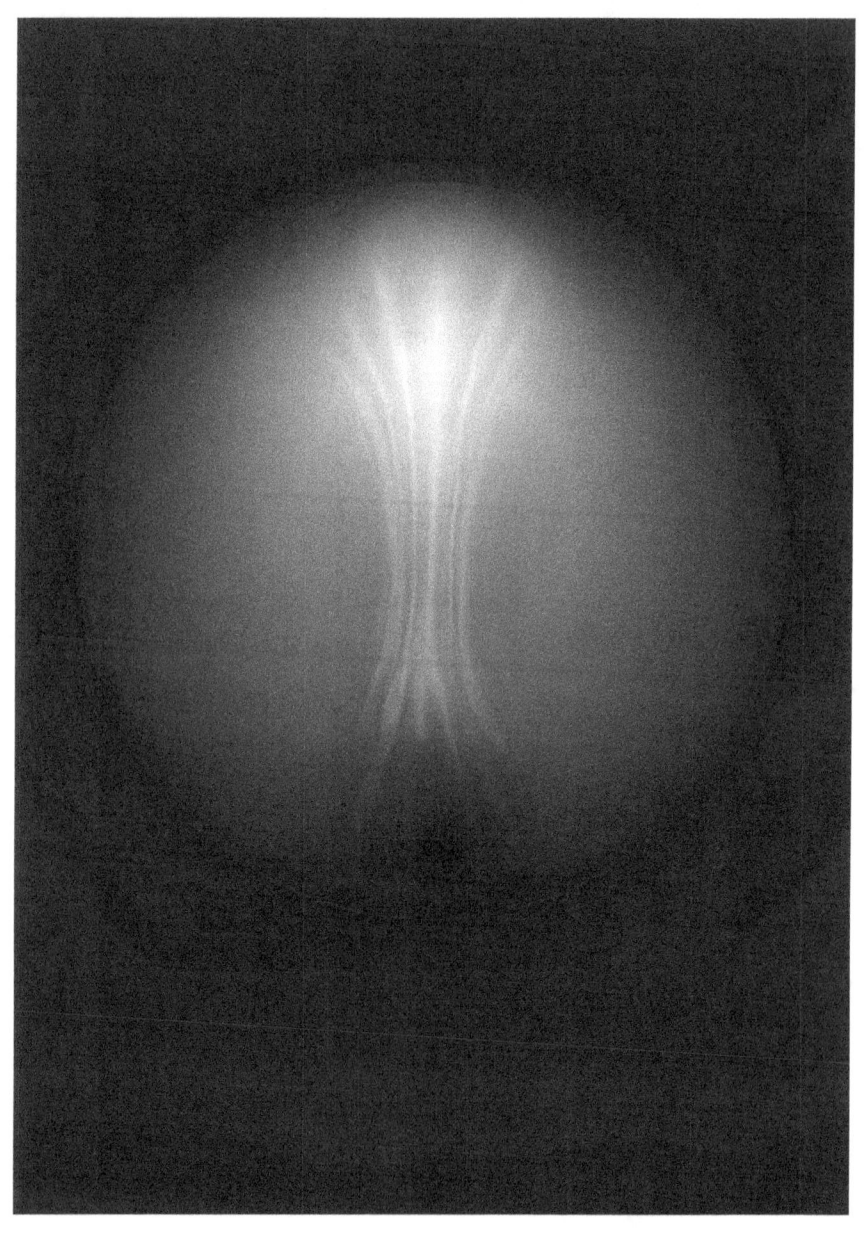

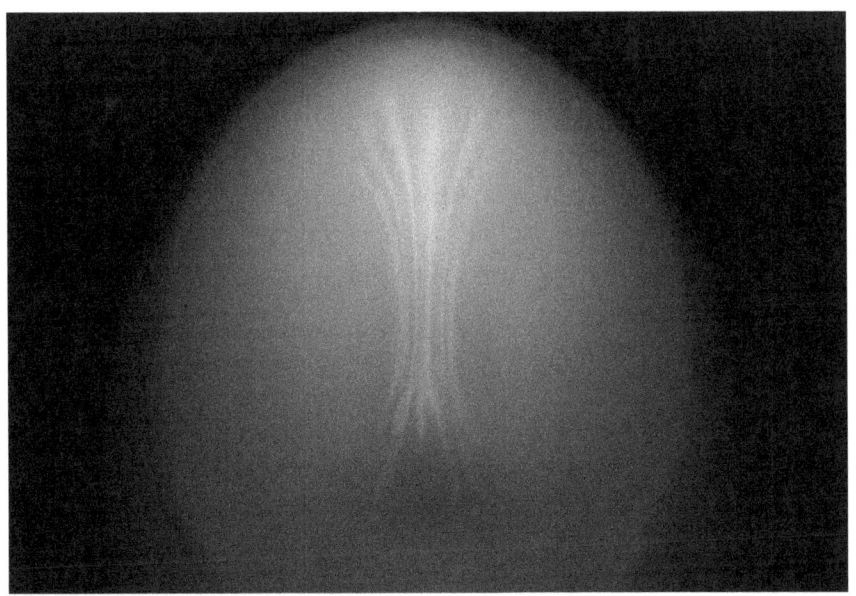
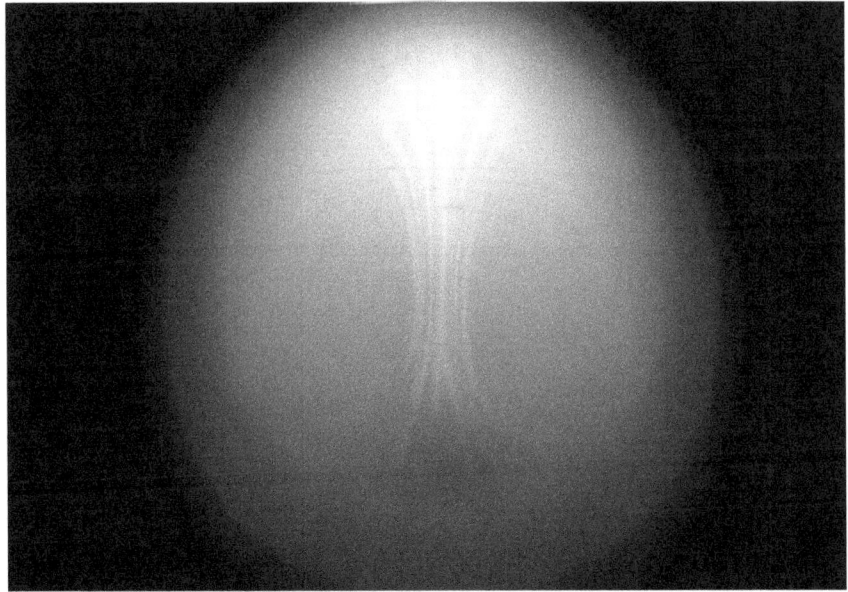

I was puzzled by many questions. What was it that I had seen? How did it hover, as it made no sound, had no wings and looked like it was solid, though transparent? Was it alive, or was it a machine, or was it a living machine? Was it from this world, from these dimensions? Was it man-made, or something from another world, another reality? Why did I see it? Was it by accident, or was it there on purpose, for me? Why didn't it communicate?

The initial consequence was my changing understanding of time and space, and communication.

Already a few years before the "close encounter" I made this graphical model to help me understand how a deeper, or larger, or higher, awareness would differ from a lower awareness.

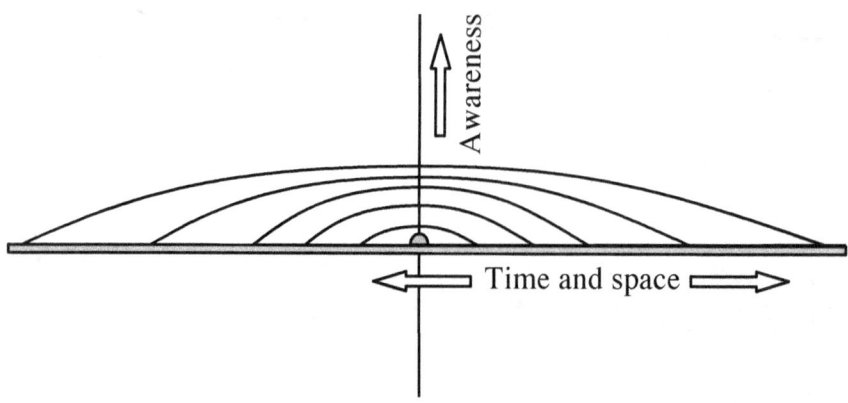

For the sake of this example we'll put a piece of rock at the centre of this two dimensional model of a 3D reality. We'll dedicate the X axis to time and space, and the Y axis to the level of awareness. The rock just sits there, it is part of the 3D reality, with time included we'd go to 4D, where it still just sits there, without awareness of time and space. Then we take a microbe, it grows, it lives, it moves through time and space, but is not aware of the space it inhabits, nor of the time it lives in. Closely related is the awareness of plants, for the sake of this example we won't discuss whether or not plants or trees have a conscious awareness. A jump higher we come to rabbits, with a short memory, described as ranging from a few minutes to a few days max. The awareness span of a rabbit therefore relates to remembering where it was "recently", being aware of day and night, and understanding the environment it is in, friendly or hostile. How would it differ from the awareness span of a horse? It is used to large spaces, and remembers people, friends and commands. Dolphins? They have a reputation for being intelligent, well-communicating animals.

So now we have a few curves in this model, where the exactness of the relative curves is not important, because where we want to go is the curve(s) of "humans".

Just as we've seen different curves for different beings, there is not just one curve that represents all humans. Different people, different curves, right?

The issue that started to puzzle me was the fact that, the higher the awareness span goes, the wider it goes. And the wider it goes, the more it seems to approach the shape of a straight line. A straight line however, a parallel to the X axis, would represent absolute awareness of time and space, unlimited awareness, a God-like state of awareness of time and space, infinity, in this reality. This means, that, because of their awareness some humans are closer to God (whatever or whoever God may be), than other humans. The difference being closely related to brain or mind capacity (whatever that may be).

Can I teach, can I train my brain, so it reaches a higher awareness span? Yes, that is possible, but then it becomes spooky. What are the limits of my brain, if I can reach the parallel, or even come close to it, what will happen to me? Will I go mad? Will I cease to exist, in this reality? Will I jump into higher dimensions?

And what happens beyond the parallel? Parallel worlds?

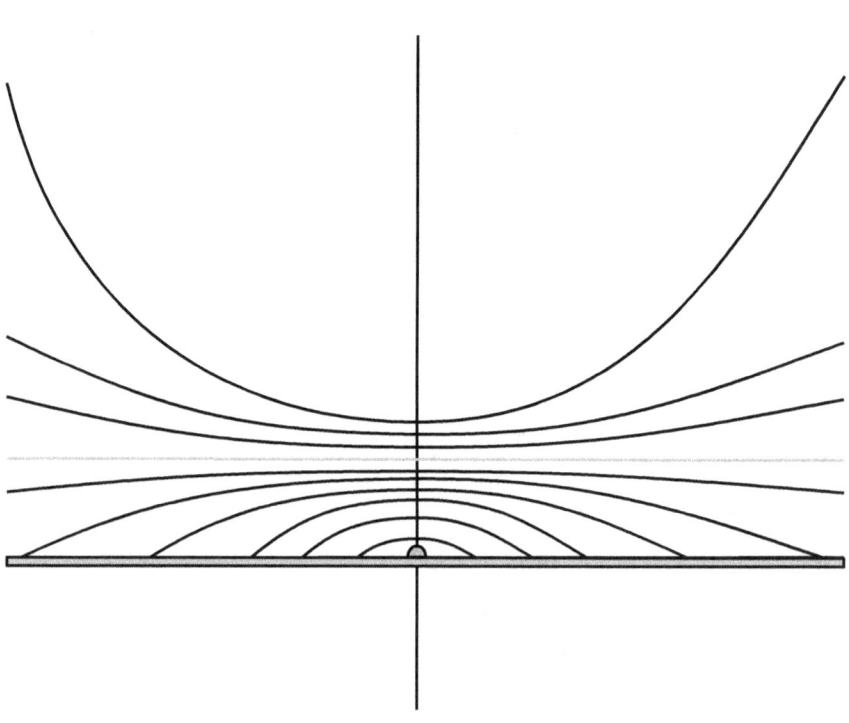

Will the parallel flip over to the other side, and in the end form into a ball shape, or a point, or will it freely form into a new shape, or shapes we've never even seen, imagined, or even considered? It also becomes very similar to another model I made, "the baseball", but for the sake of not getting distracted too much, we'll discuss that later.

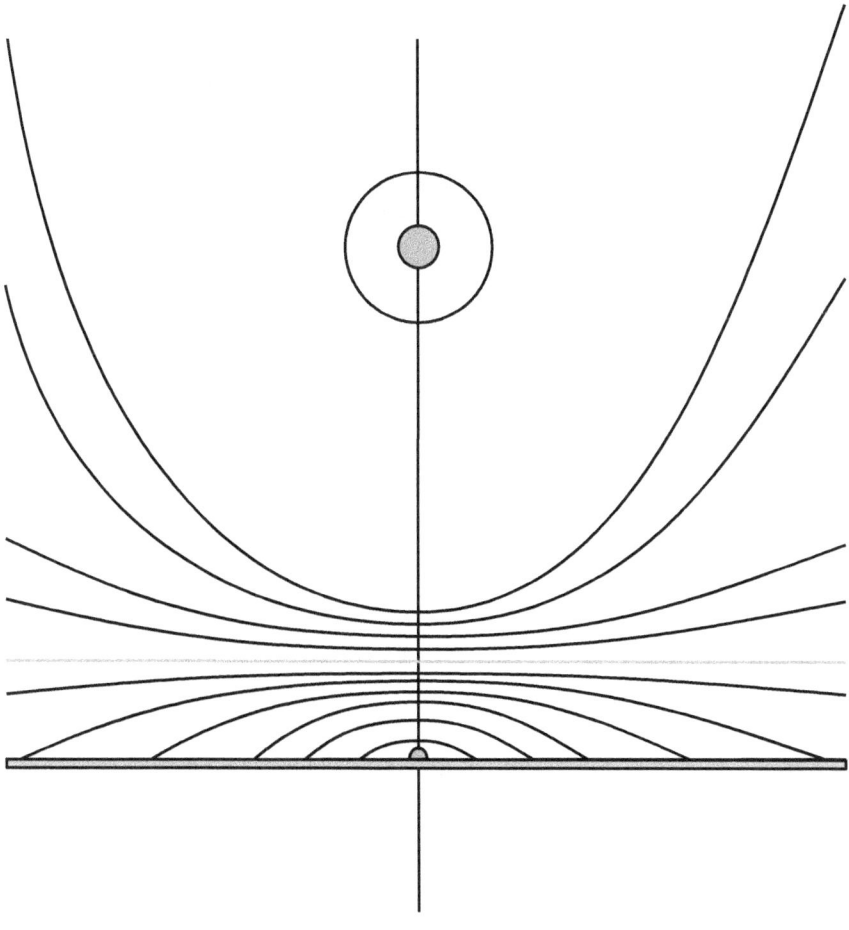

The world above the parallel line

What is the consequence of an awareness beyond the parallel? Is it an awareness of whatever is, has been, or an awareness of whatever can be? Up to, and in a parallel world, time and space seem to be connected with each other, but in a world beyond the parallel? Do time and space always have to be connected? In these dimensions there's reason to accept that, but beyond these dimensions? I think there's room to disconnect the two.

Disconnecting time and space from each other may seem unimaginable in our world, in our reality (realities), but in a world beyond our understanding, or even beyond our imaginations, I can imagine it is so. There are known knowns, unknown knowns, known unknowns, and unknown unknowns, as Donald Rumsfeld once said considering 9/11, but, as in this case, also known unknown unknowns...

While most people believe that we live in a 3D world, the reality of such a world would be a static one; no change, no life, because for that we'd at least need the 4D world, with time. But even then, is the reality of someone living in the 4D world just a 3D reality, with added time? I imagine a small group of people sitting in a room, each one of them has a handicap; one is blind, another is deaf, can not smell or can not taste, or has the connections to the brain mixed up, or has no arms or legs.

For each of these people their reality is missing a dimension compared to people who have a complete set of senses.

Smell adds a dimension to reality, as does sound, or light, or even the ability to touch something that is beyond the immediate reach of our body. The dynamics of reality include far more dimensions than just the 4D world, even for everyday life of any and all people. What a wonderful world!

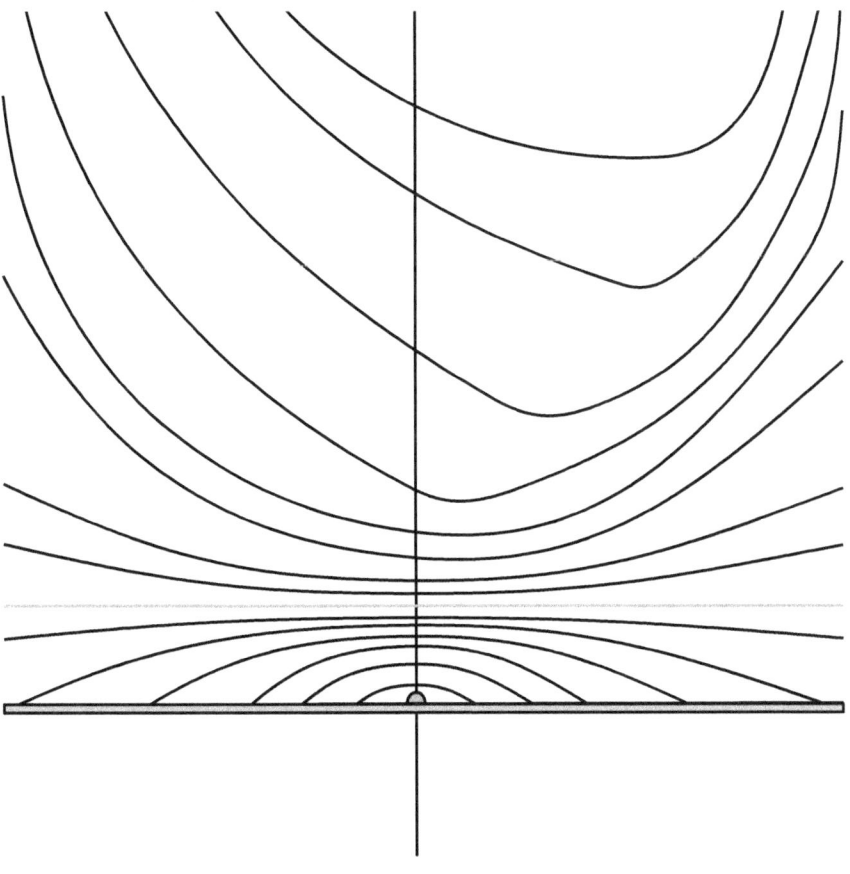

The hunt for the unseen

When Hans Martens and his son Zacharias Janssen invented the microscope in the late 16th century, they did not yet see bacteria. But one century later, Antonie van Leeuwenhoek did. So then, did bacteria exist before the 17th century, or not?

When the Hubble telescope had finished its deep field observations in 2012, it revealed 5,500 galaxies in a tiny dark speck of the night sky. Did those galaxies exist before they were found by Hubble in 2012?

When I had the first close encounter in 2008 it was just an opaque white ball, as seen during day light. But on Wednesday, the 26th of March, again during daylight, it was even closer, changed to transparent, and clearly showing a gentle light-emitting structure that reminded me of an apple core.

Because of the binoculars I could study it very closely, if only for five seconds, five very long seconds for someone who is focused. And focused I was!

Although the opaque white balls have been described, filmed, photographed, numerous times by others, and amongst others documented in "Project Blue Book" and numerous videos on YouTube, it seems I'm still the only person in the world to have seen the hovering, transparent ball, with its gentle light structure.

What does this mean?

I still do not know, but it has lead me to accept a Truth that is way beyond what we've been told since many generations. It has lead me to accept that Life and Existence can have "forms" that are way beyond our current understanding, if ever we're able to understand it at all, with our carefully controlled, limited human minds.

Why did I see it? Why did I see it on that particular day? Why did I see it when I was looking through binoculars?

Someone who responded to my YouTube picture video mentioned to me that these balls would be radioactive, if that is correct then it would make sense to keep a distance, and wait for a safe opportunity... I don't know, but it would be a logical explanation.

Does something not exist, when nobody else has seen it? The thing is, many people have seen it, but for those who haven't it is way beyond their logical understanding, or way beyond their belief, religious or not, so where does that leave us? Especially realising that I don't want anyone to just believe what I say, but to know, to understand the Truth. The Truth, I think, can not be served on a silver platter, it must be found.

Time

Time never had a beginning, therefore anything is possible, even the "impossible". How's that for a statement? The concept of time as experienced on Earth is different for every species; even when comparing different humans the span of awareness varies. Most people can feel "now", even into tomorrow and yesterday, but the longer or wider the span, the less people can feel it. But just as an athlete trains his body, you can also train your brain, and widen the span. Until it almost reaches eternity. Eternity is a parallel plane, it reaches into divine regions, parallel worlds?

Where they become parallel worlds, do they bend like the curvature of Earth, where perspective is not a straight line but flows with the shape of the globe? Does the parallel world circle around us, with us, as a spiral? As a ball?

I think M-theory can only be justified from a limited human perspective. It hints towards a reality beyond everyday human life, but then stops at the limits of its own scales, whether or not we can see them, the confinements of this reality.

What a wonderful world

Slowly, but steadily, our modern world has changed. For most people only visible through their daily affairs, brought to them by modern entertainment media, but for a few visible from their ivory towers, their personal illusions of wealth and prosperity. The wonderful world of organised crime has grown into many directions. I'd like to focus on debt, debt per capita, debt per head. Let's jump into the puddle.

The purpose of the European Union, similar to the United States of America since "modern times", is to have a huge block of taxpayers who can service a huge block of debt and become hooked into a fat system of bureaucratic control and financial manipulations that are presented as if it they are the opposite. Comparing New Zealand and Ireland, both with a population of about 4 million people, and both (having been) under financial control of American Federal Reserve, and Merrill Lynch, Banker John Key who suddenly became Prime Minister of New Zealand. From the financial manipulations by John Key in Ireland we've seen how that country fell into (created) debt, similar to all "Westernised" countries, of about $50,000 per head of the population. The financial position of a drowning Ireland being backed up by the large financial pool of the European Union.

Money trader John Key and his financial aid Bill English announced that they first wanted to raise New Zealand's debt, after which it would come down, after many years into the next government's terms. The amount of debt they talked about would be 200 billion New Zealand dollars, which is about $50,000 per capita. Similar to the debt per capita where Ireland ended up; fascinating, isn't it? To me it seems as if this $50,000 per capita, relative to the different disposable incomes per country, is a holy figure, carefully calculated in the plush rooms of international bureaucratic money controllers, international bankers, international banksters, or maybe just with a wet finger high into the air, dipped in Scottish whisky. Maybe the magic number is $66,666, after all we've still not reached total collapse of the current corrupt money system.

When we look at the debt per head in 2015, in several "westernised" countries, we see these figures, in approximate US$ (source Bloomberg):

- Ireland $60,000
- United States $60,000
- Belgium $48,000
- Italy $47,000
- Canada $46,000
- France $42,000
- United Kingdom $39,000
- Greece $38,000
- Netherlands $37,000
- Norway $34,000
- Spain $30,000

- Denmark $29,000
- Australia $18,000
- New Zealand $15,000

While Ireland was backed up by the European Union, a great safety net of tax laws and taxpayers, New Zealand is not part of such a system. So what was John Key, the international banker from the USA, doing in China, making deals about excluding the American dollar in international trade? Debt creation has several functions; one is the creation of interest, the other is control. With the creation of immense debt, they created a "legalised excuse" for strategic asset sales, and guess who have the money to spend on those asset sales?

Watch the bottom two countries go up in the ranks in the next few years. What a sad world if we let that happen; after all, we could have Heaven on Earth, as this financial system is an illusion, an invention of people who do not understand, who do not care, what a wonderful world really is. There's is no need for this illusion at all, we've been tricked into some kind of wonderful world that is not ours, or is it?

Conditioning of the minds

Marketing, propaganda, rituals, traditions, fashion, symbols and ornaments, Panem et Circenses, Divide et Impera.

What is the difference between marketing and propaganda? Is there actually a difference? One for political purposes, the other for commercial purposes, and nowadays most often even a mix thereof. When corruption is the name of the cake, who eats from it, who gets fat from it, who is making it and who is paying for it?

When I looked at Buckingham Palace it reminded me of secret portfolios, hidden bank accounts, the illusions called "royalty", the enormous propaganda machine, the smart trickery of keeping servants loyal to the corrupt system, the contrasts between the illusions and reality, the decadence that is keeping us from creating "Heaven on Earth" for all, inequality, injustice, cruelty and sheer organised crime.

Seeing who or what we're dealing with here, I imagine the late Princess Diana, being initiated in the family secrets after her marriage, and becoming aware she does not wish to be part of it. But at least she had done one part of the mission: breaking with the traditions of inbreeding in "royal circles".

When we were standing at the memorial plaque for the "The Diana Princess of Wales Memorial Walk" it did not feel as if she was there. It felt she was far away, meaning that such a walk would be just another form of propaganda, keeping the illusions alive. Nevertheless, we're all free to choose our own illusions, so I chose to enjoy walking there in her honour.

New Zealand's mining industry

It's constantly the same propaganda stories.

Local businessmen smell their local short term profit opportunities, and do not (care to) look at the long term consequences for others; and other local business men who are tricked into forming a NZ company with the foreign mining companies (for legal reasons), and will say it creates jobs.

Yes, of course it creates jobs because those corporations are not going to do the highly corrupt, dirty and dangerous mining work themselves!

And why do these local (or even imported) people choose to do that work? Because the corrupt career bureaucrats managed to keep the workforce poor, employment low, the workforce as large as possible and yet hungry for consumption and a job.

So, why do we in New Zealand still have that ultra-corrupt thing called the "Crown Mineral Act"? Because it pays 3% in royalties? What is royal about it? Ah, that royalty has a lot of shares and commercial interest in the mining industry?

Living in New Zealand

For me, coming to live in New Zealand turned out to be a huge culture shock. No matter how well I had prepared myself, learning about New Zealand's history, starting to learn the Maori language. The thick headedness, narrow mindedness, childish, immature, selfish, short sightedness slowly started to blow my mind.

A few years ago, during a party, I got into a friendly discussion with a Labour hardliner. He was proud to have met Helen Clark, "She is one of us", and no matter how or what I explained to him, and even after he said that I might be right..., "she (still) is one of us".

Adding to that, mindless "cut your lawn" culture, lack of (general) understanding of international Art, then these silly political "discussions" (they are more like statements of stubborn points of view) start to make sense.

In my "financial terrorism" campaign, directed at key figures in New Zealand politics, education was a core issue. Nobody from Labour picked it up, nobody from the Greens picked it up. Maybe I should discuss it with National? Education, from a broad and deep perspective, is immensely undervalued in New Zealand. Our education system does not make better, more complete people; it only produces the taxpaying work force that the Kleptocrats need to create the profits.

So, where do you start when Education is the long term solution, but that same education system is managed by corrupt career bureaucrats who prefer to keep it the same, even while creating the Illusion of a freer education system with charter schools. When the entire education system, from bottom to top, is legally sponsored (even out of manipulated need) by the short-term greed of the business elite, what else can we expect than change? Yes, change, but only for the worse!

When I learned to see my own blind spots, I learned to see their existence in others. While seeing them you can choose what to do with them, either accept them or do something with them, change things. Some I chose to leave where they were; they were either too trivial or too unclear for the moment to effectively work with them. Either way, they were part of my journey, they were part of who I am, and part of who I could choose to become.

Learning to see my own blind spots when I challenged myself to have an objective view of myself, for me would turn out to become some kind of awareness, a cleansing process even, however with the simultaneaous appearance of something like a depression. Mourning my losses, detaching them from the core structure, while making that same core structure stronger than it ever was before. I learned to see it more like growing pains than as suffering, or even what a depression might really be. This awareness has helped me to see blind spots in entire cultures.

Within all my American friends I learned to see a similar behaviour, unable to see their own blind spots, encouraged by the distracting amusement industry or the misleading bought mainstream media, unable to see that point of reference that makes American society like a shallow bubble, no matter how well educated anyone seems to be. It is similar, though different with the British island mind perspective. Like a defensive mind mechanism, as to preserve an entire society from going down, indifferent of its own quality of existence.

3D printing

3D printing and the housing industry, another propaganda/marketing presentation on TED that I saw in 2013. They never seem to learn, they have new technology and instead of understanding "integrated design" they build traditional houses with it. The building industry is the slowest and most easily corruptible learner in the classroom. Seriously!

About 20 years ago I started discussing a new building technology with large building companies. With my technology they could build earthquake-proof lightweight houses for 2/3 of the cost of traditional houses. One didn't want it because their 10% profit margin would mean they would make less profits (they could not think outside the box), and another company, whose executive team wanted to try it, stopped because their construction workers didn't want to get into technology they weren't familiar with.

And here in New Zealand, the one company I discussed it with, had just launched a new line and did not want to risk starting another one. Theirs was just another style, nothing essentially new. They do not understand "long-term process gratification thinking" vs. "short-term instant gratification thinking".

My personal lesson was when I designed a house for my family, and hired one of the largest architectural firms to assist me because I wasn't familiar with NZ regulations. During that process I learned about traditional building in NZ and how people do not understand integrated design. Hence they chop off the top of a hill and build a house there that could have been built anywhere. The land is not complimented by the house, and the house is not complimented by the land.

Driving through NZ I see a chain of missed opportunities, while on the other hand I see a new opportunity for integrated design around every corner.

The other thing is, when it's on TED, you always have to put it in the context of what organisation is behind it, after all, behind TED is one of the largest marketing companies in the world...

Bragging rights, and shame duty

I like the expression "bragging rights", it gives justification to stating a truth that otherwise would have been ignored for "showing off", "not done" or the typical Dutch "not being modest", the tall poppy syndrome.

During my high school time, especially in the beginning I was quite average. Growing towards graduation I started to become more aware of myself, as many did of course, and noticed that my motoric skills started to catch up with my intellectual talents, although then I wasn't aware, nor did I even remotely understand how those two could be related.

On Friday afternoons we had no scheduled classes, so me and a group of senior students who enjoyed all kinds of sports used the opportunity to use the sports grounds or the gym hall as we pleased, and quite often one or two of the sports teachers, specifically Mr Oudakker or Mrs Poelmans would join in. I think volleyball was our favourite. For me it gave me the opportunity to research and teach myself special techniques, especially for the serve. For an attack shot, we called it a "smash", the shot was accompanied by a loud bang. That same kind of shot technique I learned to use in an overhand serve. It became some kind of a dazzling mode. Over time my serve evolved into something so precise, so fast, so overwhelming that I could almost play a game all by myself against the opposing team during the regular sports classes.

Sometimes I would do that for a few minutes, then would

loosen up, so we could all play, as shame duty started to call in.

I loved baseball. I loved it. Did I mention that I loved baseball?

When my motoric skills were developing so well that I could throw a ball in a straight line into the glove of a catcher, with a better than 90% score, it was time to demand my place on the baseball field as a pitcher. In a somewhat theatrical style (that I had seen on TV) I would turn my back towards the home plate, bend forward, slightly down, bring up my left knee and turn with a catapult action. Well, that was how I saw it then, but indeed I was getting quite good at it.

So, one day, during regular sports classes, I was standing on 3rd base. Our sports teacher was Mr Kloen, who for some reason I always thought, felt, did not like me, especially since I had noticed that his daughter, who was in my class for a year, was in quite a snobby clan along with the daughter of the principal, Mr Buma. They were acting like "a different kind of people", only interacting with the children of known rich people, way beyond ordinary people, at least that's how I saw it, how I experienced it.

One particular day during regular sport classes, baseball, the ball was being hit, flew and landed in the midfield, while I was guarding 3rd base, with an opponent starting to run from 3rd base to score a point. I was yelling for the ball, but it came very slowly, and when I finally had it, "my man" was only a few meters away from the home base. I knew I could throw a ball in a straight line into the glove of the catcher, but there was someone running in between. So I stepped to the side, and in a straight line, right over his shoulder, right along his head, I threw the ball in the glove of the catcher. "OUT!" And then it was silent. "WHO did that?", Mr Kloen asked. Hesitating for a moment, feeling somewhat proud and embarrassed, I raised my hand, "I did". Then there was more silence; for a whole minute, that felt like an hour, nobody said a word, while Mr Kloen took out his little notebook and started writing. And then, as if nothing had happened, "Carry on..."

What was in that note? Who knows, if he had been paying attention he already would have noticed I had lightning fast reaction speed and exceptional motor skills, but I was someone from the out crowd, so really, in the end, who cares...

What this memory illustrates to me is the magnitude of importance of good teachers and professors, how they can make and break someone's entire life, in a good way and in a bad way.

It was the same thing some 20 years later when I had decided for a gigantic career change from the medical-pharmaceutical industry towards architectural design. Again, but this time far more personal; lack of self-awareness and personal shortcomings of the teachers came seeping through. This formed the idea that the education system should be centered around bringing forth the best of each individual student to form the most colourful, diverse and talented society possible, instead of teachers making egotistic copies of themselves. Doing the same thing, over and over, instead of evolving into whatever we can be together, making this the Paradise on Earth it could be, could have been?

The Round Table conflict

When our history teachers told us about the Round Table we were given an illusion of noble men all fighting for a good cause.

Nowadays we have our own illusion of knights at the Round Table, but now they are all career bureaucrats, no matter who or what they work for:

- government
- private or corporate industry of some kind
- a charitable organisation
- or even a religious one of some kind.

Imagine a large round table, luscious wood, thick leather seats, and a choice of drinks and nibbles prepared and arranged for each seat, for each guest. And here they come, all dressed in uniform "suits 'n' ties", the modern-day camouflage suit to make bureaucratic criminals look decent, and it worked! Now every hardworking lower-class bureaucrat likes to be seen in suit and tie (not the multi-thousand-dollar variation of course, but preferably some nylon mix with shiny spots), as to show off his illusion of success and his position in the corporation.

At the round table however, they did not discuss these matters. What they did was discuss how to find an opening in the next salary and bonus discussions for a nice raise in payments. How would they get what they want, because what they all wanted was a big raise in their financial wealth, no matter the consequences for the lower classes or whatever. As said, they needed to find an opening, the first one of them to succeed in managing a big raise to a certain level was to be the new benchmark!

Exhibit A got a salary package of almost one million dollars, but with a bonus package worth even more. So, for him what mattered was to get the results as drafted in the contract, so he would get those millions. And as every experienced accountant has learned, numbers are very flexible, and even more so are their interpretations, so you can create about every desired outcome. After all, also the truth has many perspectives.

So what happened at the round table? After Exhibit A succceded in his pay rise, Exhibit B, sitting right next to him, was appointed the next contending career bureaucrat. Of course they did not put it as such, because suits 'n' ties prefer to create a very decent illusion of themselves. And so they did. When it was his turn, Exhibit B pointed at Exhibit A, to use him as the new benchmark in the industry, and after a while he succeeded. Then it was the turn of Exhibit C, sitting right next to Exhibit B, and it already was easier to get his pay rise, after all his references had already doubled.

As time moved on, it turned out to become ever more easy for our round-table contestants to "justify" their exorbitant wages and bonuses, all approved by their peers of equal and lower ranks, because they also wanted to be in that seat at the round table. After a few years, the round circle at the round table was completed, everybody had had their turn, and we were back at square one...

This time however, with the small increase that was part of every step in the negotiations, the difference between the first and last round-table career bureaucrat had become quite substantial; a reason for Exhibit A to use Exhibit Z as his new point of reference. And so the new round began, the circle had become a spiral, a helix, all justified by other career bureaucrats.

It's a conflicting situation, isn't it?

A lesson from New Zealand

Some thoughts about my general experience, my lesson, in New Zealand when I designed my own house to make a (integrated design) statement for the new country that I brought my family to. Because I wasn't familiar with NZ regulations, I asked for assistance from one of the largest architectural companies in NZ.

In the Netherlands I would've done mostly everything myself, it's part of what integrated design actually is about. Here I needed to hire a bureaucratic "specialist" for everything, who'd have to sign off for everything, and get paid for everything. While I would be instructing one and educating the next, only the last one who came aboard I could really work with. But it seemed the typical NZ problems with building just a "better house" were far from over…

Only after coming to live in New Zealand I learned that bureaucracy is far worse in this country than in the Netherlands. Here in fact I learned that anything that the control bureaucrats can lay their hands on, they take the life out of. And it's far more serious than it sounds.

I've actually stopped dreaming about setting up a design firm in New Zealand, and the local production facilities along with it. To change it, it seems I'd have to become a bureaucrat amongst the other zombies, and they'd still have no clue what I'm talking about… except the Smiling Zombie (aka the Smiling Assassin), he would have a clue, but he just couldn't care less. But that's an entirely different story.

FIVE SECONDS

JOHN V

More education

A slogan I used years ago, during the YouTube wars, was "More Education, Less Bureaucracy", which still stands. Anything that the bureaucrats can legally lay their hands on, they eliminate its life. They want to make regulations, even if they have no clue what the essence is of the thing they're regulating. Bureaucratic control serves a dark purpose; public control and tax management under the disguise of public service.

Considering Education, the corrupt control bureaucrats have managed to streamline and narrow it down for corporate benefit. That is why I proposed S.N.A.P. to the government: Science + Nature + Arts + Philosophy, with history and sport as sustaining topics for all major departments. First I had Math only in Science, but even Math fits and sustains all departments. It was actually Math that helped me understand and make clear an essential philosophical problem of how Humans and God (or a concept of what God is/could be) actually do relate, completely void of religious humdrum.

There are things that I know, or better, understand, beyond most people's imagination. It's one of the lessons of my life, and it even got worse while growing older, simply because getting older and being open means more life experiences, of all kinds. Already when I was young I would get in conflict situations with people of authority, simply because I always ask(ed) questions. I do not accept authority simply based on position, which is also why I despise most politicians and their corruptible bureaucratic law system. People have learned to hate "know-it-alls", no matter how hard they (I) try to be modest and gentle. It serves a "divide and control" purpose for the control bureaucrats...

I've decided to do some actual reading on Plato, and not just rely on the snippets I've been reading, and already am amazed. I do not agree with everything Plato or Socrates says, but boy, realising that it was written some 2400 years ago, and how they already discussed so many essential issues about society, politics, corruption... If we had proper education, people would not allow their governments to make the same mistakes over and over, AND would have been motivated, informed to properly protest poor governments, just like they used to do.

Therefore it is not surprising that, when the Romans came to power, they introduced "Divide et Impera" and "Panem et Circenses", that we're still dealing with. For me it is absolutely clear where and what the problems of our societies are, but, I'm not a politician, and I do not intend to be one, although as a service to humanity I would consider it, if it were not that we need to get rid of this entire political system, the whole thing; actually politicians are exactly the kind of people you do NOT want as a government.

Plato, Socrates

The greed of the unrighteous man is determined by the extent to which he differs from a righteous man.

The cause of each injustice is weakness. Because at any attempt for cooperation they will bring hatred and discord, first by weakening the cooperation and then by making it disappear altogether. The power of the mind is Justice, injustice is its fault. Thus it is that, through Justice, the mind has an excellent ability to think about things, to lead and to live happily. But when Justice disappears, the outcome is the opposite. Government should be made of honest people of high moral standard, with no conflict of interest, with an army out of highly trained people (body and mind) without (corrupting) material interest, regulated by law.

And what do we have now in our modern world? Why is our education so poor that people are not educated in essential philosophy, with essential understanding?

When Socrates states that it's better for young soldiers to be informed with happy stories concerning death and the "underworld", it's a statement of corruption. For soldiers to be able to be cruel he states that they should not worry about their "legal" victims and therefore only show them specific sections of Homer, and leave out the ones that could cause doubt. On the one hand they want soldiers to be well-informed, well-educated, well-trained and well-balanced for their jobs; on the other hand they want to decide what that "balance" looks like, which then can only result in quite a deformed idea of balance. In fact, what they discuss is brainwashing, and how to justify it according to their restricted rules.

When wise people make sensitive remarks they should not be quoted as such, Socrates states, to prevent young people from thinking that it's good that people are caring, sensitive or thoughtful. Instead Socrates wants them to be in full control and (seemingly) cold-hearted, especially considering soldiers.

When I look at today's society I see the exact same concept, but then used widely in our education system. University students are not encouraged to find their own way, but they are manipulated into courses that corporations want them to do, and corrupt university boards are eagerly willing to assist. So, modern students are in the same boat as the brainwashed soldiers that Plato describes; the only difference is the battlefield.

Money

Money was invented as an instrument to make the barter system work more smoothly. There was nothing wrong with it. I think it went wrong because of (at least) these two or three issues:

1. The invention of interest, and its legalisation by corrupt governments.
2. Money became a goal in itself. By collecting just money, it goes out of the system, leaving less money to go around between people and therefore decreasing general prosperity.
3. Fiat money.

In a different world, where people truly understand love, there is no need for money. People would enjoy caring for each other, people would enjoy spending time for each other, people would enjoy sharing etc. This joy is selfish, just as selfish as the greedy, consumerist, materialistic society we have now, but it is deeper, whole, connected to the Oneness we all are, no matter the different dimensions we live in.

My dream for now would be a revolution, where interest is abolished in any and every form, including the fake different prices in Muslim countries for cars that are paid cash (low price), or cars that are sold without initial cash (high price). Governments have the legal power to create a credit system for their entire population that would provide a benefit for everyone, in many ways. The other essential part of that dream is a legal limit to money/wealth collection. Nobody needs more than a certain amount of money, and the excesses are just theft from humanity, from global prosperity. After all, we could have "Heaven on Earth" for all.

Of course everyone should be open to this discussion, but helas, not everyone is motivated to be informed; the current misguiding system tells people that just having an opinion is good enough to participate in any discussion, which reflects the modern illusion we call democracy…

Surely everybody has a right to their opinion, but not everybody's opinion has the same weight, and therefore should not have the same voting power as someone who cares to be truly informed. Looking at our societies it seems that that is exactly why we have the current system, because propaganda and marketing techniques still work: "Panem et Circenses", "Divide et Impera"… The more voting power to the misinformed and uninformed, the easier an entire society is corrupted, which sadly illustrates our current societies.

Traditional design

Considering the chapter I wrote in my 1997 thesis on old houses, and traditional design in new houses, I've actually come to dislike the new fashion of "traditional design", because it influences people's thinking in a traditional and rigid way. It is a constant influence on people's minds because they spend so much time of their life there. Imagine an open mind, and how it would design a new house, and imagine a closed mind, and how it would design a new house. It works in many ways.

Does that mean that all new, modern(ist) or contemporary design is good? Far from it. Both in traditional and "new" design I have seen well and poorly integrated designs; most however are poor. When houses become very expensive they also grow in their coldness and ugliness. The exceptions to the rule are only by designers who understood "proportionate design", like Frank Lloyd Wright, or Le Corbusier, or Ludwig Mies van der Rohe, or Baragan. A few years ago I studied some 500 houses and (then) found that beyond a price tag of about NZ$600,000 houses start to become ugly anyway, meaning that the most interesting houses had a price tag of about NZ$500,000 to NZ$600,000. Prices in various Anglo-American countries are changing quickly, but the principle remains.

It seems that in that price range people have enough money to spend on a house, but also have to consider spending it wisely and are informed enough to often get the help of good designer, which there are not many of...

Interest, mortgages and investments

This is a little story that the banks, real estate agents, and car dealers will not like. We've all been manipulated into the illusion that we need to own a house. Upon this illusion we've been manipulated that we need to have a certain kind of house. A house with a specific style, in a specific neighbourhood, a house that represents who we want to be, or better, the kind of person we want the world around us to think we are. Similar issues are with the cars we drive, the right size, the right brand, the right style, the right amount of bling.

And all of that comes with a price. When you're caught in this game, chances are you'll go for the maximum effect, meaning you'll go for the largest mortgage you can afford, along with the most impressive car in your garage. When you've been saving money, you can cut down the amount of money you need for a mortgage. And after a while you'll be able to pay off more and more of that mortgage. After a while you can see your percentage of ownership grow, and mostly you'll still be paying a similar amount of money per month, for interest and to pay off your loan, the mortgage. And after many, many years, you can finally say that you own the house.

But, the amount of money that you've invested in your house is stuck in that house. You can say to yourself that your house is now interest-free, which is not true. Every day that goes by, you are losing the interest that you would have gained if the money was invested in an interest-bearing account.

With houses it is possible that such a loss is "balanced" by inflation in the real estate market, or even by financial inflation itself. The market manipulations we've seen in recent decades, however, make that assumption a tricky one. Some people can afford the gamble, others can't.

Quite different is the story with investments in cars. Let's take a middle-class car, with an investment of $50,000. Once you buy that car, let's say new, and drive it out of the dealer's yard, the biggest depreciation will happen, and after that the relative depreciation will slowly become smaller. Your used car is costing you a fair amount of money for maintenance, replacing parts etc. and therefore a new car looks interesting.

The investment in that new car however, will cost you the interest on the entire investment for the rest of your life...

Every year you will lose out on the full amount of interest on the initial investment. Let's say 3% of (deposit rate) interest on $50,000; this means that every year, for the rest of your life, you're paying $1,500 on interest on that car. Yes, for the rest of your life. And that is apart from the interest you might even be paying on the car loan they'd been selling to you.

In short, while investing in real estate is a gamble, an investment in cars is a definite, huge loss.

All thanks to the financial system we've all accepted as being normal, because the Bible refers to interest as being normal. In reality however, interest is the biggest scam of all.

To put this story in perspective let's name a few other financial scams of all sorts and styles: currency trading, national and international taxation, levies for government services (that you didn't ask for), shares, privatisations and their abuse of public property (historic and/or contemporary public paid investments like energy production), stock markets with their own inventions of financial gambling and risk diversion. In the end, in this (corruptible) system, the taxpayers always pay. And while the illusion exists that the richest people pay the most taxes, in reality it is and always has been the middle class that takes the bulk of the burden. And it's always the middle class that greedy, selfish government bureaucrats target with their tax and control system.

Imagine what would happen if the middle class would be well-informed, well-educated, healthy and happy. Would they take all that shit that is happening around them and around the world? Would they sit back, hope that things don't change so nothing serious would happen to their huge investments that they took out huge loans for? Or would they stand up against the abusive system?

The news anchor Howard Beale comes to mind, from the movie "Network", 1976.

"First you've go

t to get mad..."

Legal banking illusions

The first illusion was PAPER money; then, after a long while, they created ELECTRONIC money, with which they created full control of our salaries to ensure we'd pay the full profits (interest) on the fashionable illusion of mortgages.

Politicians were happy to support the idea of electronic money, because it also would help them to collect taxes, especially those paid by the middle class, where the bulk of tax money comes from.

Then came the illusion of PLASTIC money, which was to introduce total control RFID chip money. Illusions upon illusions! And if that wasn't enough, they made marketing campaigns for people to have RFID chip implants. And after many decades "1984" came, and it was worse then we ever could have imagined.

The global banking illusion

The concept of INTEREST is the crux. There is no need for interest in the money supply! It is an illusion, a brainwash.

Every country can create its own money and therefore give a loan to every citizen to build a house, without interest.

It's that simple!

There is no healthy balance in a corruptible system managed by corruptible career bureaucrats for corrupt corporations and corrupt aristocratic illusions.

Receiving huge amounts of interest for doing nothing, for pushing a few buttons on a computer, must be the biggest scam ever, after the organised religions. People believe it's all justified, people have been made to believe it's all justified.

Not the Dutch mountains

Everywhere I look, in any direction, high or low, I increasingly see how the bureaucrats and their corrupt system screw up our societies. I'm actually at a point where I sometimes tend to look the other way, as the corrupt issues are becoming like a mountain, and I'm sure it can not be the purpose of my life to build my own mountain(s) to climb.

In "The Republic", Plato contemplates about who dies the happier person: the corrupt man with an illusion of justice built around him, or the just man who has to fight for every inch to expose the truth and the lies...

Reading "The Republic" has already confirmed many, many issues in today's world that I found/learned by myself. I imagine the learning curve if I'd been taught it at an earlier age, but do realise that when you're older you understand things differently, meaning I might not have understood what I understand now, the structures, the patterns, all the perspectives, micro and macro. I can see through all of it, and indeed they are mountains. But I can move through them, see what they're made of, hm....

Surely I can move mountains.

The meaning that each and everyone gives to our lives, our existence, is an illusion, meaning that "The Matrix" is closer to reality than just a movie.

What if existence on Earth is Heaven and Hell, and everything in between, to learn, evolve, based on previous "lives"?

What is it?

What is the purpose of Life? The purpose of Life is to give meaning to Existence. Then what is the purpose of Existence? In essence, there isn't one. Then what is the purpose of accepting this pain, this cruelty, this bullshit by the global organised criminals, the corrupt career bureaucrats and their corruptible control and law systems? In this infinite existence, in all of its dimensions, without beginning, without end, this could be Heaven, Heaven on Earth. So again, why are we accepting corrupt(ible) laws, corrupt aristocrats and their corruptible bureaucratic law system, their corrupt career bureaucrats, all of it, to ruin our existence?

So, if there is no purpose to Existence, why are we here? The most logical answer to that is to sustain the corrupted system (in all of its dimensions and/or forms) that our lives exist in, and with that ALL life that exists in no matter what forms or dimensions. We have given meaning to what, in essence, has no meaning at all; in other words, it's all an illusion. So again, and again, why are we accepting an illusion that is causing so much pain?

If it's all an illusion, then why shouldn't I go kill myself and by that prevent all the pain in me? This is exactly the point where organised religion had to be invented. If all of this illusion is to sustain a corrupted system, meaning a corrupted existence, then indeed "they" needed to invent a way to keep the masses that sustain this existence alive and happy to be so. Hence, organised religions, with a great illusionary reward hanging in front of our lives. And if you're going to take that reward away from the masses, they're not going to like that; even worse, some have been programmed by their organised religions to blissfully go and kill you, since you're not from their religion. Isn't that unbelievably smart? Or is it just evil? Organised evil? Organised crime? Or what exactly is it? After all it's an illusion, isn't it? Or is it?

TIME never had a beginning, humans are just a little speck on the reality of existence.

This reality is one of many possibilities. THIS is the reality we have to deal with.

JvZ©2013

When my son was 7 years old, he said in the supermarket: "If you don't buy that chicken, the next chicken won't be killed". That's the day we became vegetarians.

The fact that existence never had a beginning and that existence has no purpose is a conflicting reality, a contrast of gigantic proportions. Being an architect and to make "eternal" monuments, therefore has no purpose. It's kind of useless. It's like the "zero-point" of our existence. Is the "zero-point" in the middle of a circle, a sphere, or is the "zero-point" in the middle of an X-shape, moving from contraction to a (new) expansion? (First inward, then outward, in one direction) Is the "zero-point" in the middle of endless amounts of "Klein bottles"?

Beauty

Let's look at an Orchid, form follows function AND form dictates function, meaning form=function, and function=form. Beauty is also a function, but there is shallow beauty and deep, intrinsic beauty. Beauty from the inside out, and beauty from the outside in.

Beauty
without charm
only pleases us,
but does not hold us;

Just floats along.
Useless, a bait
without a hook.

Capito, 55 BC

Good vibrations

Smell, taste, touch, sound, light; all different ways to deal with different manifestations of frequencies and waves. Imagine, if these already are such amazing ways to deal with frequencies, and yet are so "normal" for us humans, what else could be possible for which we don't even have words, yet?

When there is no sound in space, then Earth must be (like) Heaven. When everything is "frequency", a specific tremble for specific particles, like electromagnetic waves, light waves in a wide spectrum, then the "invention" of sound and its receivers, ears, was a great addition to all the other senses. They made Earth, as if it is "Heaven". They gave us Freedom, as if it is Heaven, they gave us Choice, as if it is Heaven.

Then there was Emotion, Love, Caring, and Choice. We could choose Emotion, Love, to Care, or we could choose to be cold-hearted, like a reptile, without Love, not caring about anything but oneself. Heaven and Hell are here and now, but most people choose not to see it...

Democracy

Democracy is a precious, complicated thing on the one hand, and just awfully simple on the other.

You can choose; you can make it a system that seems fair, because every person has the same voting power, like one person-one vote, but, in the complicated mix of corruptible bureaucratic laws and carefully constructed marketing/propaganda the masses (of votes) are too well-distracted from proper information, or even proper education, that the one person-one vote "democratic" system has been carefully manipulated as to make the voting a simple one-liner popularity contest.

For a proper democracy it is needed that each "one person" has a specific minimum of understanding of the world he/she is living in, and that specific "minimum" relates to education, which has been hollowed out during the last decades to just produce the taxpaying work slaves that the corrupt "elites" want; and information, which as we all know by now comes from bought media, who have to deliver the (entertaining, distracting, disinforming) message that their owners/shareholders or advertisers want.

Democracy should be precious and simple, each one person taking responsibility for one's own well-informed vote, and self-motivated to vote, because the system would be inviting. Our education, information system is far from that; the old Roman "panem et circenses", meaning in today's world "give the people food and entertainment" as a numbing drug, and "divide et impera", which in today's world I'd translate to "divide and control" still are the backbones of our controlled, corrupted societies.

2400 years ago Plato and Socrates, told us about it, the risks, the systems, the abuse; hence "The Republic", or philosophy at all, is not part of our education system, because imagine what would happen if we'd really have an informed one person-one vote system...

Why do we have this illusion, called a democracy?

Because the majority are sheeple!

JvZO 2013

Move

When corrupt career bureaucrats (aka politicians) around the world create any and all laws to "define" terrorism, but avoid to define "financial terrorism" it should be pretty clear where the corporate and private lobbyists are spending their time and money.

With more corrupting laws it will only get worse. Sheeple will wait for each other to take the initiative, to take responsibility, and most probably will do nothing essential. They are like frogs, waiting for the water to boil.

The answer can not come from the sheeple, the herd is carefully numbed and many of them even might get angry if you'd try to wake them up...

How to move the masses then? Ripple effect, snowball effect or domino effect? Will one change ripple through societies? Will one change grow along the way and cause more and bigger changes? Or will one change be the start for others to automatically follow?

Plato, once more

Plato wrote in the Republic: "And the different forms of government make laws democratical, aristocratical, tyrannical with a view to their several interests; and these laws, which are made by them for their own interests, are the justice which they deliver to their subjects, and him who transgresses them they punish as a breaker of the law, and unjust. And that is what I mean when I say that in all states there is the same principle of justice, which is the interest of the government; and as the government must be supposed to have power, the only reasonable conclusion is one principle of justice, which is the interest of the stronger."

Plato wrote that 2400 years ago. Have we learned yet? Nope, our corrupted education system does not teach that in case we would learn and do things in a different way, more humane, more healthy, more equal, better, good.

What if New Zealand is not the least corrupt country in the world, but the most corrupt country in the world?

The greedy slave-drivers said that time is money, and the tax-work-slaves believed it.

War

The glorification of war, it's an illusion, it's propaganda, it's marketing, it's corruption. I'm sick of people falling for the propaganda illusions (created by the war and media control industry), labeling war victims as "heroes". Never in the history of mankind, a war has been started for the people, but it's always the people who pay: either as taxpayers or with their lives, as civilians or as soldiers.

MIAMI INTERNATIONAL AIRPORT
February 1993

My (then to-be) wife and I were waiting to collect our rental car, when suddenly a young woman walked up to me and asked: "Excuse me Sir, are you someone?".

A week later, we got married as planned, the whole bureaucratic way, from Miami, Dade County, to Kissimee, Osceola County. "Kiss me" as we called it.

Apocalcatalyst

What can I say?
The Truth would blow your mind. Would it pop more gently if I told it slowly? Or would you prefer to read it in a book? More vast, so you can see the slow-motion picture leading towards "The End"? The Big Bang, after all it's just in your head.

The system

Here's how the corruptible bureaucratic law system works:

- They make a set of rules, and call them "the law".
- When you beat them at their own game, they just pull out another set of rules, and/or refer you to another department.

I can see through it so clearly, its transparency is like water, and they think it's mud they're spreading in our eyes. They don't see it coming, but their misleaders do. None of them understand it though, when they think they do, as is illustrated by their actions.

I can see the "Game Over" screen coming in their game. They do not understand how they could have missed it, when it was right in front of them all the time.

Facades

False fronts (commercial, religious or government) are here in many forms, and they all work in the same way: 1. They attract as many people as possible by telling a story in a way that many people like (marketing/propaganda). 2. When they have a certain amount of people, a threshold, they start to change their policies. 3. The people that have been hooked will be re-directed (typically narrowed in) in a specific, pre-planned way, for either commercial, religious or societal control/political reasons.

"Sometimes I wonder whether the world is being run by smart people who are putting us on, or by imbeciles who really mean it." Mark Twain

"I am free because I know that I alone am morally responsible for everything I do. I am free, no matter what rules surround me. If I find them tolerable, I tolerate them; if I find them too obnoxious, I break them. I am free because I know that I alone am morally responsible for everything I do." Robert A. Heinlein

The propaganda-marketing machine

When they bought the media, they bought the words and changed their meaning, stuck new manipulative labels to them, so people would lose their original constructive meanings.

Education, proper education, is the key to solving the problem; probably that's why it upsets me when people who professionally teach other people have no clue about life, its essence, and no clue that they have no clue...

We need complete education that connects everything to everything and guides people towards constructive answers, instead of controlling them to just find the little information that keeps them stuck in this controlled system.

In a way we have such a long way to go, while on the other hand it could be changed by tomorrow...

Religion-chance-evolution

Considering that time never had a beginning, we've had endless realities before us. Do we need something like a god to have (created) this existence? With endless time, and endless trial-and-error realities we could have come where we are purely by chance, without a creator. With endless time, we've most likely been here before, doing the exact same thing, or something slightly different. 1,000,000 years ago? 1,756,345,245,459,678,456,234 years ago? 7,584,947,657,858,696,868,679,785,930,937,598,367,587,577,464,577,854,949,272,885,490,958,984,503 years ago?

Endless time, no wonder humans came up with the idea of religions, isn't that far more convenient than trying to understand the truth? And then mix in some controlling laws, et voila: the herd is ready.

Before that, endless possibilities for intelligent design from different dimensions, where the higher or highest dimensions refer to what people now call "God". Intelligent design and evolution, to me, are a logical mix, but not something to be manifested in a religion. The concept of "believing", or making people believe, is what keeps societies under control.

The god of organised religion is a control instrument.

The religion of money

Money is an illusion we all came to believe... They told us it was backed up by gold,... which are two more illusions, as gold is just a yellowish metal and the money isn't really backed up by gold, as the entire financial system is an even bigger illusion.

Someone, somewhere, makes a lot of profit from illusions, and with those profits buys up "the real world", the world of castles, aquifers, islands, factories, mountains and just land, lots of it. However, even that "ownership" is an illusion, a legalised illusion, because with the corruptible bureaucratic law system, they created an illusion of Justice, an illusion of justified ownership.

We all came to believe that everything "they" buy is their justified possession, because the law, that was created to serve them and control us, was made for them, not us. While, and because, the financial system is continuously sucked dry by the financial merchants, the people are kept under control. Their wealth is constantly minimised, just high enough to keep a society from revolting, just low enough as to keep them in fear of "poverty".

Money has become a semi-god of a destructive illusion.

Control

10 years ago I'd never have expected me to defend gun ownership, but learning from history I certainly do now. However with that I also "defend" information, education, as to make people wise(r). Informed, educated, healthy and balanced people will not choose to use weapons unless there is no other choice.

The current global chains of command are corrupted to the core, and they abuse their "legal power" to disarm the people they want to control. It's a similar issue with the "government" spy agencies: the corporations want all information for "security" and "surveillance" (which actually means control of the opposition), all paid for by the taxpayers!

All control instruments are being used and abused against the people of our global society. People are constantly bombarded with all kinds of distracting information which keeps them from seeing that the actual global divide is "corrupt versus the rest". So information and education are crucial; hence the strategic, organised hollowing out of both by the corrupted governments. From taxpayers' money they have organised global control instruments like the World Trade Organisation, the United Nations, the International Monetary Fund, and the World Bank to create a facade, a nice-looking legal front, for people control. Add to this the FiveEyes (FVEY) spy machine that is completely growing out of control, and it becomes clear that humanity is under severe attack.

Humanity is under attack from within, like a cancer, affecting, infecting and taking the life out of everything it can lay its tentacles on. For the sake of Humanity, we need to keep and maintain our defence mechanisms against the global cancer. Firstly with proper information and education, but, if needed, also with guns.

"They" are preparing (again with taxpayers' money) robotised control and warfare, because robots have no conscience, they do not care, need no salaries, have no families attached and can be continuously produced. The Cancer will use everything they can against the Human Body. The Cancer will not choose to be healed, it will not heal itself, so WE have to remove the Cancer, entirely, with all of its systems and networks. Only then will we be able to create the Heaven on Earth that this place can be, where guns will be our last defence against any other cancerous attack from within Humanity.

A patsy is born

Listening to a radio show a few years ago, I heard the host mentioning another shooting (in the USA) where a young man went on a shooting spree, killing 6 people of which 4 were men. The alleged motive would have been rejection by women. In the following years more shootings would follow.

I thought about a pattern; to me it seems that from a certain point in recent time a rhythm, pattern, started. Something like "bizarre shooting-quiet-bizarre shooting-quiet-bizarre shooting-quiet etc.". I thought about the concept of patsies, about the "Sandy Hook" shooting and its actors, and the "Boston Bombing", even about JFK. Then, I realised how a mass spy "surveillance" system, collecting all data they can get their hands on (electronic medical files, shopping (both online and in the 4D world), financial information, tax, emails, phone calls, tweets etc.) and all in "real time", can easily be abused to create patsies.

"Anything that can be abused, at some point in time will be abused".

We already have the corruptible bureaucratic law system. It will be abused, because it can be abused as for corruption you only need two things; a corruptible system and corruptible people managing it. At this point the spy system is managed by the corruptible system, that is managed by corruptible managers; career bureaucrats, both corporate and government. Then put the two together, and we get this:

A spy agency that collects all data, and only has to filter out one particular person that fits a specific profile. From another angle they can create an event, like a shooting, that can be "perfectly linked" (an illusion) to a specifically selected target, based on the collected metadata and the selected profile. A patsy is born, a pattern of patsies is born.

Now, seeing these bizarre shootings, and its intense rhythm at a time where the controlling government wants to disarm its sheeple, it is perfectly possible to create any event and tailor-make it to fit a spied-on patsy. It's so easy when you have the (spying) instruments that the patsy doesn't even have to be there, while the corrupted (bought) media present the perfect illusion for the desired effect, which is taking away the people's right to defend themselves against a corrupt control government that is growing out of control, and has been doing so for quite a while already.

New Zealand's corrupt education system

Our entire "Education" system is strategically hollowed out, following American and British examples. Private schools attract double funding (private and government funding) and pull away the better teachers from public schools. Charter schools will create more polarity on both ends of the social scale.

This way a typical "British" social "divide and control" system has been created, where one group with some financial wealth enjoys showing off their illusion of status, and the other group with less money will not be able to provide their children with "better education". The stigma of public and private schooling imprinted in children's minds, on their way to a future divided and controlled society. "It's not real" they'll say, "It's in your mind", and yes, they are right..., well, it's real, and it's not real. The illusion is unreal, its consequences are real.

All this distracts from the intrinsic problem of education, where students are not educated to become better humans, as individuals, or to become "more complete", but instead to better fit in the carefully controlled taxpaying work slave system. Some slaves will push this system to be enhanced, well-funded, all out of cold-hearted self-interest. Inequality of the lower and middle classes will be the visible norm for political division (divide et impera), keeping the real divide with the extremely financially wealthy carefully out of sight. Looking a little deeper, and we would see the entire illusion of the money system, that has been accepted as fact of our existence, just like an organised religion...

Directly derived from the Old Romans, with their "Panem et Circenses", New Zealand has a pride in their "sports culture", another illusion where a few make big money as pawns (like the gladiators) in the modern gambling and entertainment industry. Sports as a broadly adapted sustaining grassroots activity is perfectly healthy from any perspective, but as a major subject in education and society it is destructive for the long-term well-being of a prosperous, healthy and balanced society.

Education now is deprived of its deep and broad potential beauty, and only offers the cold molds in which the corporations and corrupt controllers want their workers to be formed. It's a global problem, and it will only get worse if we do not stop it entirely. In other words: students with huge debts that they can only repay by becoming a workslave for the same companies that lobby the universities and control the programmes that are being offered as to get the workforce that they want, in the way they want and for the price (cost) they want to pay, by keeping the supply higher than the demand.

Business

One of the partners in a local lawyer firm (Hamilton) told me that 80% of their business was against the local council. Imagine the cost to taxpayers and ratepayers for the council's lawyers. Imagine the ongoing costs for the public, paying for both sides.

Then imagine a world without the corruptible bureaucratic law system, where all money is truly productive, constructive, a contribution to the well-being of humanity instead of sustaining the expensive suits and ties (private and government).

It seems very logical to me that a certain group of lawmakers and policymakers do need to keep this system intact out of self interest, or worse, make it grow for growing profits, with ever more bureaucratic control organisations.

Who would benefit from that, apart from the bureaucrats?

School control

Recently I had a discussion with a (religious) school principal, who said this: "Rules are to control people; without control, you get anarchy". This made me aware that rules, in a healthy society, should be to guide people.

And as such the difference between the "10 commandments" and the Georgia Guidestones became more clear to me. If, and I mean IF we were to write something down for humanity, as a guide (!), to me it could well be something like those Guidestones.

> - Maintain humanity under 500,000,000 in perpetual balance with nature.
> *(yes, why not? Does this mean we have to kill off people, or have a natural flow towards it? Of course, IF 500,000,000 makes sense, then it should only happen in a natural way, without any form of violence, and over a long period of time.)*
> - Guide reproduction wisely — improving fitness and diversity.
> *(yes please)*
> - Unite humanity with a living new language.
> *(Hm, a new Esperanto? Not so sure about that)*
> - Rule passion — faith — tradition — and all things with

tempered reason.

(A balanced, healthy mind?)

- Protect people and nations with fair laws and just courts.

(Moral Justice instead of the current "corruptible bureaucratic law system"?)

- Let all nations rule internally resolving external disputes in a world court.

(This is exactly as I discussed 20 years ago during philosophy training at the art/design academy)

- Avoid petty laws and useless officials.

(Yes! and in a different system altogether.)

- Balance personal rights with social duties.

(Balance is a dynamic word, not static...!)

- Prize truth — beauty — love — seeking harmony with the infinite.

(What can I say? Of course!)

- Be not a cancer on the earth — Leave room for nature — Leave room for nature.

(Isn't that fascinating? To me that relates to how I describe the cancer that is ruining this world, formed by the corruptible bureaucratic law system, and its corrupt(ible) career bureaucrats).

The Bible, Exodus.

I am the Lord thy God

Thou shalt have no other gods before me

Thou shalt not make unto thee any graven image

Thou shalt not take the name of the Lord thy God in vain

Remember the sabbath day, to keep it holy

Honour thy father and thy mother

Thou shalt not kill

Thou shalt not commit adultery

Thou shalt not steal

Thou shalt not bear false witness against thy neighbour

Thou shalt not covet (neighbour's house)

Thou shalt not covet (neighbour's wife)

Thou shalt not covet (neighbour's servants, animals, or anything else)

New Karmaland

A new karma for New Zealand? Putting things in perspective, with one prominent politician after the other turning out to be a fraud, what does that say about New Zealand's political spectrum?

Never in my life did I live in a country where lying comes so naturally to people. People in every profession, from all walks of life. It is so natural that corruption is part of the system, and because it is part of the system, outsiders can not see it. Hence Transparency International thinks we are about the least corrupt country in the world. But since living here I have come to quite a different view; in countries that are openly corrupt, you just know what to expect when you engage in business or any kind of official negotiations. Here in New Zealand it is all hidden behind Old Boys' Clubs, and old Colonial Networks, even referring to the bureaucratic illusion called "royalty".

I say, New Zealand had it coming. New Zealand had it coming since the very first beginning of the bureaucratic colonial exploitation illusion under a corrupt flag, we're not even United Tribes under this corruptible bureaucratic control system. Corruption thrives, and it serves a purpose, that of "divide et impera", or as I would say it "divide and control". Corruption thrives, because we have cold-hearted, greedy controllers in legalised controlling positions. Corruption thrives, because people are afraid, and why are they afraid? They have been beaten into submission by constant media control, the constant beating of war drums, the constant theft of public assets, the constant threat of an increasing spying network in the spirit of Orwell's "1984".

A country that has everything to be Heaven on Earth, but is carefully controlled for short-term profits and exploited to the hilt without caring for the long-term consequences to the Nature of this country. I say, such a country has it coming.

I say, Karma is a sweet revenge.

Time II

Time never had a beginning, therefore existence never had a beginning. There can never be an end, there can only be change. Change is the only constant. Therefore, one can not go in circles...

Time is change. Change for the good is growth, is differentiation and integration. Change for the bad is death, is disintegration and decay.

- Integration is the process of becoming one, whole.
- Decay is the process of becoming a similar particle, like the rest.

"This universe, which is the same for all, has not been made by any god or man, but it always has been, is, and will be an ever-living fire, kindling itself by regular measures and going out by regular measures." Heraclitus

Beauty II

When a discussion arrives at "to each their own", there's not much more to achieve. We do not "see" whatever we want to see, we can only "see" what we can see (perspective, direction, dimensions, depth, layers etc.). One person's sky is the other person's closet...

Different skies, different limits, different properties, different possibilities. We do not all "see" the same realities. I see the space around me with my eyes, my ears, all of my senses and my mind. I feel space, very direct, its beauty and its ugliness. Very often I have to close myself off as a form of self-preservation.

Words like "Zen", "Minimalism", "Organic" etc. have been abused in modern times by fashionable designers and the mainstream media they cling to. They form the core business of (popular) modern shows like "Great Designs" and most design magazines.

Good design is not aesthetical (appearance), it's ethical (from the inside out). Deeper is wider is better.

One of my mottos for both my life and design philosophy is "I do not compromise, I only settle for the perfect mix" (out of respect for the Beauty of this Existence). It brings with itself a greater responsibility for being informed, with everything you do (active/passive), resulting in a deeper respect for everything, as to not waste materials and effort where they should not be, or should be different, to maximise their intrinsic values, while having clear senses for beauty and ugliness. And no, Beauty is not in the eye of the beholder, it's in their hearts and minds, or it is not. Most people have developed very little of it, but are great at mimicking popular beliefs of beauty, that actually just are fashion.

FASHISM

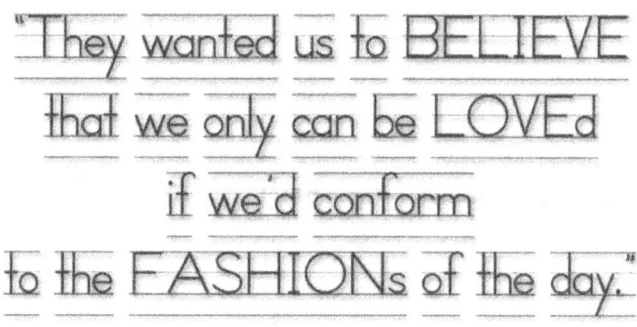

"They wanted us to BELIEVE that we only can be LOVEd if we'd conform to the FASHIONs of the day."

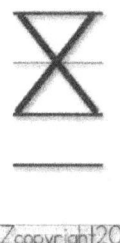

JvZ copyright 2013

Choice education

Better education means better choices, not just more choices. Therefore, if control bureaucrats manage to hollow out our education, they will be able to more easily manipulate our choices. Considering TPPa, TTIP, TAFTA, TISA etc. this means that corporations of all sorts will need to dictate what our education encompasses. Already now we see that hollowing out, to provide the industries with the workers that they need. People do not learn to "work to live", but they learn how to "live to work".

While the amount of products to buy may have become endless, our choices have become manipulated into one direction: buy more.

Buying has become our only choice, even in or for our leisure time we need to spend money: buy. But the hardest thing to accept is, and with that to close the circle, more and more we have to buy our personal education. More and more we buy into accepting that it's normal to put ourselves in great debt, to be able to have the choices in our lives that we want.

So can we choose to either have a good education with great debt to be able to have the great choices we want, or stay poorly educated and have poor choices? They are both incorrect, and both correct, all at the same time, and that means that the political market for illusions is wide open. We can be persuaded to believe either this, or that, depending on the (manipulated) situation we tend to be in. Our choices are not really our choices anymore. Just as well as logic dictates the best choices, the lack of proper information to make the best choices has become the driving force in the wide markets. We think, we believe, that we make free choices and that all of it just is a matter of logic, that there is no other way we could choose than to choose the way we do or did.

So again, I see how education dictates the quality of our choices, and from there I see the importance of free education, and with that the importance of a wider education like described under S.N.A.P.

Better education and free education is what we need, as humans, as humanity. Without it we're doomed to fail.

With the current system our evolution narrows down towards the future; with free and better education our future evolution spreads wide open. The drone operator who chooses to do that job to pay off the debt from his expensive education, and the mercenary who went off to exciting distant places, with better and free education could have made different choices. The drone operator could have become the constructive, creative engineer he always wanted to be; the mercenary could be an adventure camp operator, somewhere deep in the mountains. The possibilities with free and better education are endless, but what we have now narrows us down to the path of doom.

What would you choose?

What would you choose to do for it?

What would you choose to do for it, if you were free to choose?

Meeting the hovering Orb on a mildly cloudy afternoon in 2008, and what came from it

First I was amazed, of course, it confirmed that what I thought I had seen a month before in my pictures was real. It confirmed that further research was essential. I found many videos on YouTube that showed opaque whitish gently glowing balls, hovering through the sky just like in the first pictures I had made. But none, and even to this day in 2017, none showed a similar transparent ball, with a gentle glowing "wire" structure in it like I saw it in my close-up, close encounter in 2008. In simple terms, what it showed me was that "Life is More". Life is more than what we had been told for generations by corrupt governments, corrupt organised religions, corrupt organised criminals of all sorts.

To my surprise it took me deeper into a realisation I had ten years earlier when I had written a poem (in German), and discussed it with Lindsay Crouse, during that lunch meeting in Oakland, California in 1997. Lindsay was on some kind of mission, she said, seeding productive thoughts of awareness.

The conclusion from our discussion about who I am was:

Life is More.
I condense the Essence through Feeling.
And push the Limits, to reveal the Beauty of Life.

Back to the orb, and the realisation that Time and Existence never had a beginning.

What if Earth is just a gold-mining colony for a species or a form of being that is not human?

Considering that time never had a beginning, and therefore Existence never had a beginning, this means that Anything is possible.

If anything is possible, then why are we so obsessed with a yellowish kind of metal that even our organised religions glorify it as a materialistic object? What is the logic of spending huge amounts of money and effort in mining for gold, and then melting it into blocks to stash it away in vaults?

It is logical, considering that time never had a beginning, that somewhere in time "a species" found out they needed gold for their survival and learned how to create a different species (that we now call humans) that can do the collection of gold for them on this planet, in the endless Universe.

It is not the only possible explanation for why we are here and now in the state that we are in. But it's a logical one that carries in it a perfect solution of how to get our Earth back in shape towards the "Heaven on Earth" place it could be, for everyone! That is why it is worth it to see from every perspective. Actually, that is why it's essential to see from every perspective.

Banksters

When loan documents are bundled and securitised weekly by our local banks, these mortgage banks, selfish loan sharks, function as a self-serving front, a facade, for the global organised criminals who created the bureaucratic illusion that is the current tax, debt and control system.

When mortgages are being packaged and sold to third parties, that is where the hidden global organised criminals (a mix of new and old big money) stay out of sight for the general public, but also for lower-class public servants who do not see the wide and deep criminal financial scheme crawling over the entire globe.

These "third parties" or even "fourth parties" are the names we find related to the creation of the fake American "Federal" Reserve Bank and their Federal Reserve Act, for which several American presidents already died, for trying to stop the cancer from growing.

Choose Wisely

With every hour passing, it may become clearer how cold-hearted Israeli Organised Terrorism already was a strategic basis for 9/11. With every more destructive step they confirm more of a brutal pattern, a brutal cold-hearted strategy.

This must be the most brutal criminal organisation ever, again, using religion as a basis for alleged superiority.

I'm not a religious person, and the way I understand what "God" is, is miles apart from what the scriptures try to make people believe; but, or maybe even because of that, I have an understanding of what love is, that most of religious people are missing. They all say, they all believe, that God is Love. And yet they cheat, kill, rob, disrespect, steal, as if they are doing the right thing.

> Do they really believe that a loving father could ever kill any of his children?
>
> Do they really believe that a truly loving father would love any of his children more than the next?
>
> Do they really believe that a truly loving father would control their lives so they do not experience the most of it?

If they do, they truly have no clue what Love is. If they do, it shows the power of the written word, propaganda, marketing. It shows how a lack of personal responsibilities leads to dependence on what others tell you to do, to believe, instead of taking responsibilities for the quality of your own life, as is what Heaven on Earth has offered us all, as are the consequences for each and every action we take and do not take.

Caring and sharing are actions of Love, they are joys of Love; hence, what is happening in Gaza, in Israel, has nothing to do with Love, has nothing to do with God. Do we all get what we deserve? Do we all get the Love we deserve? Freedom is a choice. Freedom is a choice for good or bad. Freedom is a choice for love or hate. Freedom is a choice, to simply believe, or to go the more difficult road of understanding. Freedom is a choice, to follow the leader, or to take responsibility for your own actions. Freedom is a choice, for love or hate, for good or bad. Freedom is a choice.

Choose wisely.

Bureaucrats

In modern history there seems to have evolved a need for bureaucrats. Where did that come from, and how did it evolve into the corruptible bureaucratic law system we have now, with all of its criminal consequences? Why would mankind spend their precious time collecting data and processing it in a control(lable) system?

Governments should be serving the people, guiding them, not controlling them.

The slow transition from public service to public control had not been noticed; people were busy consuming, being entertained, being scared. Public servants have become public controllers, corrupt public controllers, in all Anglo-Americanised countries.

Free Americans, what has become of the illusion?

It's fascinating to see the typical organised "Divide et Impera" positions building camp in about every American political discussion, Democrats vs. Republicans, left vs. right, progressives vs. conservatives, with the help of some good old manipulative, suggestive ignorance.

There are several layers, several points of view to all of these discussions, but most are ignored to select one single layer, one isolated viewpoint, just to make an immature divisive point, whether about organised religion, financial control, organised debt creation, the war industry, the security industry, the oil industry, the re-building industry, the surveillance (spying) industry, the media industry. All of them appear as manipulations both in time and place(s).

Since when is being "competitive" similar to trying to destroy your opponent, no matter the consequences, no matter the fairness of the attempt, no matter the costs, long term and/or short term, both for individuals or societies, or even the world? Since when does "freedom" stand for "free to destroy", "free to steal", "free to kill", "free to mislead", as a justification of a selfish goal? Since when is not the entire population on this Earth one and the same family? All free to share, free to care, free to enjoy, with each other, not at the cost of each other.

Really, what does it take to have Americans take their heads out of their Democrat/Republican ***** to see, care and understand about the real world around them?

The richness of this Existence, this reality, the feelings, the experiences, you can not have that in any other reality.

Nothing is as it appears. The way it appears is how it is presented to us by the globally bought media. They keep us entertained with Putin, with Obama, with Trump, sometimes even with Cheney or Snowden, but leave the deeper, older layers "hidden" as they have created this ring of distraction around them.

Pushing up interest rates protects/serves "old money". They will still have the funds to buy property and rent it out (as it is relatively expensive in New Zealand to rent a house). Having more buying candidates in the market could push the prices up for the "old money" investors. Clearly they have the most interest in higher interest rates.

Hoarding wealth is stealing from Life/Existence itself.

Im Westen nichts neues.

Debt problems

The creation of national debt was/is to create interest income for the banksters. Debt has gone so high that they even create extra debt to pay for the interest. Isn't that cleverly thought out by the banksters?

So now that the US dollar is about to reach the maximum exploitation level (debt ceiling), they organise the inevitable switch to a new system, and start anew. And the poorly informed people will believe it to be the "solution" to the problem...

Guess who created the problems in the first place?

If we keep raising the debt ceiling, will it come down louder?

JvZ©2016

Globalisation

Globalisation goes hand in hand with organised corruption, at all levels; in fact it is extreme organised crime.

The driving forces in the East, the West and the middle are the local flavours of institutionalised corruption, the local traditions, the local histories of privileged families, castes. The Eastern models growing towards the Western models, the Western models growing towards the Eastern models, all combining the worst from one system with the worst from the other: extreme organised crime, total control.

The trend since the second World War was showing old traditional models of corruption, whether in India, Russia, China or Japan, would grow towards the Western capitalistic models, and the Western traditional models would grow towards totalitarian control models, increasing their intensity with Global, centralised organisations, fronting as for the benefit for all, but behind the curtains functioning as facilitators for private-profits corporations exploiting the illusions of benevolent global government institutions. From a globalisation point of view the East, Middle and West "grow" towards a middle ground that keeps the local colours and flavours intact as to provide a traditional familiar basis for the structure that forms the infestation; a globally driven exploiting, manipulating and controlling force, that is the violent, cold hearted, divisive, amusement park, that reflects our current world.

Globalisation has become the dirtiest mix possible of capitalism and totalitarianism in pots specifically prepared for each main culture. Local ingredients, local flavours, local traditions in a fast-food corporate marketing mix.

> While the Anglo-American empire is waging **WW3** through their war industry, costing trillions of dollars to the taxpayers and millions of human lives, China is waging **WW3** through the global real estate market with no costs but profits for their citizens, but leaving a trace of homelessness everywhere.
>
> JvZ©2017

I think the future will show us there are beings (not related to race) with a dysfunctional mental condition that have the appearance of humans, but actually are more reptilian than human.

They have the cold-heartedness of reptiles, they have the predatory behavior of reptiles, they have the short-term interest of reptiles, and they could not care less.

Never choose to believe, but know, and then learn to understand, and then travel towards the Essence of our Existence, far beyond the structures that have been put into our minds, that in essence are the Box that keeps our minds closed.

The plane! The plane!

Imagine a 2D plane with two inhabitants, in the 2D plane. They look at each other, and then suddenly out of nowhere the 3D-4D Hand comes through their 2D plane. First they see in the 2D plane the imprint of 5 fingers, then morphing into the arm, and out again. "Fuck, did you see that? I think I saw God!"...

The next day, we see the same two 2Dimensionals somewhere in that same plane. One of them walks away, and they say goodbye to each other, polite as they are, when suddenly the 2D plane folds into a circular band. They are unaware of it happening though, they can not see it changing. And in an unbelievable way, almost from one moment to the other, the one walking away finds himself behind his friend, who turns around and thinks his friend to be involved in some strange magic, or even a disciple of the miraculous God? When time and 2D space move on the circular band and form into what we can see as a ball, a bubble, but they can not see that in their 2D world, it's just a magical world where suddenly you can be behind what you were moving away from. The powers at work are too overwhelming and over time they slowly start worshipping that unintelligible, unbelievable, powerful being, which over more time even gets a following and forms into what we would now call a religion.

Then, as if things weren't incomprehensible enough, one day the circular plane transforms into a Klein bottle. There is no escaping from it anymore, the religious doctrine is everywhere. While the comfort of their religion does not explain the logic of their reality, at least it gives them peace of mind until groups start to form: one group admires the Hand-God, and the other group admires the Folding-God. And even in the 2D world, politicians, religious extremists, cold hearted career bureaucrats, self-proclaimed royalty, start to encourage groups one way or the other, as to empower their own position in the 2D world.

Then again comes the Hand and sees the 2D world, how it changed into a bubble, and the Hand picks up a magical needle, contemplating what it will do with it...

The One

There is not one Creator, as all is One, so we are part of the Creator, and the Destroyer, and everything in between, around it, and far beyond. Our Reality is one of many, and even each individual Reality is one of many more. Existence, as a whole of Realities, consists of many layers, many dimensions, where being in a "higher reality" allows you to look, see and understand "down", whereas looking "up" from lower Realities keeps higher Realities "hidden".

The difference between Life and Death, in this Reality, is like two branches from a tree, one dead, one alive. One disintegrating into "similar" particles, the other differentiating, growing, into specialised and integrating cells.

The other way around, humans becoming more of the same is similar to a dying process, and a society being vibrant and differentiating is similar to a living, growing process.

Donald Rumsfeld

February 2002: ".... as we know, there are known knowns; there are things that we know that we know. We also know there are known unknowns; that is to say we know there are some things we do not know. But there are also unknown unknowns, the ones we don't know we don't know." Missing in that statement are the "unknown knowns", because of lacking awareness and/or lacking understanding.

Party politics

I'm against party politics, because it is an immature, divisive way of dealing with essential problems, it even is a "justified" way of not dealing with them by misleading towards non-essential issues. Popularity issues and Mainstream Media have become an intrinsic part of party politics, worsening the gap between what a government should do, and what it does.

The man

There are many possible scenarios, and each of them can turn in different directions at any moment, now, tomorrow, in 100 years, in 234,364,867,473,678,934,145,798,034 years... When you understand the realities of this Existence, it makes you wonder why people choose to believe there's "a man" coming to save us, so they can stop taking responsibility for their Existence, our Existence. We are the divine being, we are part of a divine being, a higher reality, we "only" have to create a "substantial" collective awareness. We are One, but we're also still too fractured.

In New Zealand, a few years ago, we had a political spy and control crisis just before the elections, and our ("American") bankster Prime Minister John Key was involved. As New Zealand is a member of FVEY, it had the potential to make the first rip into the canvas that is the illusion that has been pulled over our eyes. The rip never happened.

The divide

People have been talking about "the divide" for ages. Rich vs. poor, black vs. white, religion against religion, man vs. woman etc. While they all have truth in them in one form or another, the essential divide I was seeing until recently was: "corrupt vs. the rest".

More essential, more pragmatic, would be to find the cause of why there is this basic global divide. When you look at how the human brain is constructed, with evolutionary parts grown/integrated onto each other, there is a fundamental difference between the earlier Cerebellum, and the newer/younger Cerebrum. The older part of the brain, the Cerebellum, relates to the reptilian phase in Earthling evolution.

The behaviour of reptiles, being cold-hearted, aggressive, careless, predatory and selfish is very similar to the way our greedy, corrupt politicians and corporate managers operate and force their world onto the rest of us humans.

Just study reptilians, both the human and the animal kind, and see the similarities in their behaviour. Then wonder why no corporation or government has ever published any research on it, while the evolutionary distinction between the Cerebellum and the Cerebrum has been accepted for ages. My conclusion is, there is an organic divide, a divide caused by a distinctive difference in the hardware in human minds.

The connections in the brains are different for each individual. Albert Einstein, for instance, is known for his huge Corpus Callosum, the connector between the left and right brain, which effects a specific quality of thinking, a specific form, or phase, of integrated human brain. With the Cerebrum and the Cerebellum, we have a connection in a different direction, top-down, a presence or absence, in different gradations, of integration.

People are more, or less, integrated.

J.F.K.

If we can study the light of distant stars, many light years away, we could use mirrors to stretch the distance of travelled light. We could SEE who killed John F. Kennedy.

One

The first royalty, as we know them in modern times, needed their tax collection to be organised, to be administered, so they invented a small circle of bureaucrats around them. In time, around these small circles of self-proclaimed royals, with their illusion of being "royal", grew a larger circle of aristocrats, feeding themselves off the privileges given by royalty to keep them loyal. These aristocrats also had their own circles of bureaucrats around them, and slowly these circles of bureaucrats grew into a self-seeding, self-serving, self-feeding, self-promoting body of organised bureaucrats, mixing government bureaucrats with corporate bureaucrats, much like the last pages of "Animal Farm" by George Orwell. The Surveillance State is managed by Control Bureaucrats.

However, alongside the royal illusion was another form of administering organisation, growing all over the world. Organised religions, they also had a deeply organised force of bureaucrats, collecting all kinds of data, spying data, controlling data, tax data and contracts of all sorts.

If we go further back in time, a few thousand years, the Egyptians wrote down their administration with the use of controlling bureaucrats but, connecting the dots, their "royalty" was similar to "gods". The Sumerians had a society where royalty and gods and religion were rolled into one. To add another dot, in modern Egypt we can still see the Faravahar, "the winged disc", which to me refers to the hovering light orb from my 2008 close encounter.

> Everything is One,
> everything is connected,
> related,
> more or less integrated.

Understanding

To create an understanding, describing opposing positions helps from within our divisive cultures. But for understanding the reality of this multi-dimensional existence, I've stepped away from just opposing positions, there's not just this or that to the same argument, there's a multitude of positions, in a multitude of forms etc.

For many years I was deeply involved in the so-called YouTube wars after 9/11. We learned there were organised groups of government/industry "shills" but also a fanatic group of ignorant followers of the "official story". They will not change, because if they did it would mean that most of their life was a lie; everything they told their children, friends, partners, in essence was a lie. Most people can not handle the truth.

For myself, as a reflection instrument, I'm aware that I've been lucky. I'm intelligent, have a deep and broad education, and have a smart, kind and highly educated wife and we have a mutual understanding of the importance of encouraging each other to "grow".

And to top that off, in 2008 I had a close encounter with a plasma light orb (one month after I had first seen it), it appeared at my home to show itself in a state that I have still not heard, seen or read about from anyone else around the world.

All of this combined gives me the opportunity and understanding that this Existence now is more than what we've ever been told, and still are not being told. I understand that I can not "save" every person, and therefore choose to only "educate" people who choose to learn. When they're not ready, they're not ready, which sometimes is hard to accept, but you have to, for yourself and Existence.

Understanding gives (a deeper) meaning to joy. My dream is a world that has abolished the (corruptible) bureaucratic (control) system, and has grown towards a more mature, healthy, prosperous-for-all "Heaven on Earth". I do not believe in anything; I choose not to believe, but to know, to understand what this world is, what it can be; a Heaven on Earth, for all. And I know we can do it. And although I do not yet understand exactly how, I know and understand that it only takes a first step to start any great journey. Let's bring this world back towards a great journey.

The first steps. Done.

I am
what I speak.

*The golden age of design
was between 80-20 years ago,
and slowly got killed by marketing bureaucrats.*

Global organised corruption

China and Russia are moving towards the Western (Americanised) model, and the Western (Americanised) countries are moving towards the old Chinese and Russia state/corporate-controlled model. Somewhere in the middle we'll find the One World Control Globalists, the New World Order.

H. Goering

"Of course the people don't want war. Why should some poor slob on a farm want to risk his life in a war when the best he can get out of it is to come back to his farm in one piece? Naturally the common people don't want war neither in Russia, nor in England, nor for that matter in Germany. That is understood. But, after all, it is the leaders of the country who determine the policy and it is always a simple matter to drag the people along, whether it is a democracy, or a fascist dictatorship, or a parliament, or a communist dictatorship. Voice or no voice, the people can always be brought to the bidding of the leaders.

That is easy. All you have to do is tell them they are being attacked, and denounce the peacemakers for lack of patriotism and exposing the country to danger. It works the same in any country."

To vote, or not to vote

In New Zealand, during the 2014 election, more people did not vote (40% of the potential voters) than people voted for the winning party (29.7% of the actual votes), who won for that reason with an "absolute" majority. This means that when you strategically discourage people who would potentially vote for an opposing party from voting, you'd create a situation where the active voters would artificially create a (false) majority.

In New Zealand, therefore, from 2014 to 2017, 30% of the legal voters got to rule the other 70% in about 100% of essential matters, including the ones that create a loss or burden for future generations. Cold-hearted, greedy and selfish voters get to create a society that gives them a short-term profit, no matter the long-term costs to the entire society.

This is not a democracy, this is an illusion of a democracy, and this illusion is legally upheld by a predatory colonial exploitation party. Would they be interested in repairing the legally unjust situation? Of course not, they are only interested in keeping the status quo, and exploiting it even more. Keeping the sheeple happy by keeping them entertained, poorly informed and scared about their pensions and mortgages. "Panem et circenses", "divide et impera". It's a global issue, a global strategy, and no global organisation is addressing it, because they've become part of the problem, they've become part of the veil that is pulled over our eyes.

The wars, the banking failures, the oil disasters, the climate manipulations, the water pollutions, the privatisations of national assets, including energy and water, it all is part of a global plan. A plan that is a continuation of global exploitation and people control, all for the same purpose, all for the same people, who only are a fraction of a percentage of the global community, and who formed a comfortable, protective layer of corrupt and greedy people around them, who do the dirty work for them, and they too have another layer under/around them who do the really dirty work.

    The structures are embedded in a "legalised" bureaucratic framework that is continuously growing, with ever more hiding places for ever more exploitative opportunities. So, which of the scared, entertained, numbed, poorly informed, poorly educated sheeple ever has the opportunity to learn to understand all of this? Almost none, and the ones who do, or try to, are regarded with suspicion, all according to plan, as Herman Goering already explained after World War 2.

Greed is good?

Does history really repeat itself, or is something else at stake? Are we there yet?

The global financial mess we see today is a result of the legal and personal acceptance of the old Wall Street slogan "Greed is Good", which has spread like a cancer around the world. It has put people in political places who should have never been there in the first place.

We have accepted "financial engineering" as a normal choice to study, just as "structural engineering" would be for anyone who'd like to design buildings, but we failed to see and understand how "structural terrorism" brings down a building, just as "financial terrorism" brings down a global financial system, for private, short-term greed, with of course deeply felt, long-term consequences for the rest of the world, the so called 99%. In reality however it's only a small fraction of a percentage, a very small fraction, that instigated the mess upon us, more like 0.0001% than a full 1%. And the spin-off, far beyond the 1%, is seen in a circle around them; the wannabes, also hoarding financial wealth, taking from the potential for a "Heaven on Earth" that this place could ever have been, for all.

We are educating financial terrorists at our public universities at the cost of structural engineers and designers, for which the consequences are deep and long-lasting. We are hollowing out primary and secondary education, aligning it with the wishes of corporations, and again the consequences are deep and long-lasting. For future generations poor education lays a poor foundation, as does rude exploitation of natural resources, exploitation of corrupted legal systems, exploitation of taxpayers, exploitation of fear. "Greed is Good"..., right?

Why and how can it be legal that we accept cold-hearted, greedy people as our governments in the first place? People who do not represent "the people" but rather the corporations that sponsor them? Corporations that are owned by... greedy people. We're going in circles, we're spiralling down in circles. While some of us are celebrating on waves of undulating wealth, others are drowning with them, holding their breaths in bitter sorrow and pain.

When "God is Good", it seems some of us have made it their religion to take everything from us, from the entire global society, to keep us from prosperity. Why? Because they can. Why can they? Because they have made us believe that bureaucratic law, their written law system, equals justice...

There is no justice, there can not be justice, in a system that is managed, controlled, sponsored, written, manipulated by derivatives from the Financial Terrorists from Wall Street. A system that feeds in on itself, legally fed by its taxpaying work slaves, its legalised corporate and elitarian exploitation, its cancerous growth and manifestation in all controlling governments and corporations, local, national and international alike.

The latest trick, the new stage, the next level on their

agenda consists the T.P.P.A., T.T.I.P. and T.I.S.A. corporate-government control contracts, and their (new name) variations to confuse the people even more. Shrouded in secrecy, even after they'd be signed and made into corporate control laws, they are ploughing their ways into Orwellian global societies, making the Old Roman "Divide et Impera" and "Panem et Circenses" controlled societies look like a Kindergarten play field.

Enough is enough, or is it?

INSTEAD OF A
WORLD TRADE ORGANISATION
WE NEED A
WORLD PEOPLE ORGANISATION

STOP
GLOBAL ORGANISED CRIME

JVZ©2015

Objection!

Being objective means either incorporating all perspectives, or none. Both do not work in a human society; there's always a shift into one or more directions, the balance is never two-dimensional, it is never even static.

For true Justice we have to be able to move through time; different aspects have different meanings in different times.

We have to be able to judge the crimes that are committed today and are protected by dodgy, corrupt legislations; legislations that are designed by corporate lobbyists, legislations that were designed to uphold the wealth of royalties and their inner circle of loyal profiteers, legislations that are designed to legally "justify" the exploitation of Earth, of Humankind, of Existence, for the benefit of a few cold-hearted beings that only have the appearance of humans, but at heart are cold, ruthless, without warm compassion.

It is impossible to have rulers, a government made of cold-hearted beings and expect them to care for the best interests of the people, for the best this Existence could be for all of Humanity, for Earth. We need a radical change, before it is too late for our children. We need to change it now.

That should be our object, real change, and not just the words, the illusions, the propaganda marketing that career bureaucrats feed us with, day in, day out; not the illusions of change, but Change, for the good of all Humanity.

What do you want?

The money changers, the international trade and financial manipulators, their shareholders, the legalised thieves of humanity, they are the scum layer of the global society, sucking out prosperity for their own stinking existence. Just because they legally can, they suck billions upon billions out of potential constructive productivity to hoard money and waste it on immense materialistic exposure.

They steal from humanity, and yet humanity has been corrupted through its corruptible bureaucratic law system to legally let this happen. And many, far too many people accept that because it is the law, it is legal, then it must be good. They believe it is good, it must be good, because it is the law; they believe it as if it is a religion, just another organised religion. And by believing that, they believe they are doing the right thing.

No, the law is not by definition good; as history teaches us, it even has nothing to do with Justice, since it is written by and for a small group to keep the modern time sheeple controlled, and give the corrupt ruling classes more freedoms. The bureaucratic law systems we have now are an illusion of Justice.

Money as an instrument to make exchange of goods and services easier is abused for criminal purposes, but because those activities are legalised, people do not see or understand they are crimes. Especially since it's been going on for ages already, and with every new generation they find new ways of stripping societies one way or the other, via big taxpaid projects, enormous bailouts, fat bonuses or in the invisible global stock trading and currency trading markets.

Traders have an interest in discrepancies, hence they have their corrupt politicians installed to keep these global discrepancies intact. And locally they sell the stories to the people, that the situation is handled, altered, controlled, in the interest of the people, but nothing could be further from the Truth. Gambling is a core issue in international financial trade, gambling and predicting the changes in discrepancies, fencing off their personal risks, with risk control, no matter the costs to societies. Would it be in the interest of such billion-dollar traders, gamblers, risk quantifiers, to manipulate markets anywhere, everywhere and all the time? I bet you it is!

The Truth, the Essence, is always at the same time very complex and very simple. We can try to understand all the different forms of illusions, the latest derivates of derivates and other poisonous concoctions, the large scale financial manipulations and dirty propaganda marketing techniques, but we also can simply say a thief is a thief. It's not hard to understand, really.

What kind of world do you want for your children, a world run by thieves or a world managed by talented, well-informed, healthy and caring people? We need a structural change.

In New Zealand we need an independent investigation to check how and when John Key (the American banker who suddenly became a New Zealand politician at the very specific moment when international financial engineering and trading was leaping into new dimensions) was (before and after he became Prime Minister) involved in manipulating (direct and indirect) the New Zealand dollar and interest rates for international financial engineers and traders of all sorts. Currency traders made millions shortly after John Key became Prime Minister...

To that we need to add the privatisations of strategic national assets and legalisations of mineral exploitations for foreign investment traders, as is happening in all more or less corrupted countries.

What do you want?

Five seconds of Truth

I wish everyone could see the Truth, the absurdity of this world not being governed, but controlled, by a thin layer of cold-hearted reptiles, predators in a man-made world of illusions, lies, propaganda marketing. A world that could have been Heaven for All, but has been made into a hell for many, far too many. I wish everyone could see the Truth, feel it, if only for five seconds.

The problem is that our governments are manned by shareholders in a corruptible, financially engineered system, who are not interested in creating legislations that recognise financial engineers as the financial terrorists that they really are. They are not interested in the Truth.

And they even are legally allowed to be shareholders in a system that they create all "boundaries" for, to prosper for themselves, not for the people and the country they're supposed to govern. So why would they be motivated to create laws that would hurt their financial prosperity? After all, whatever projects or laws they'd create, it's always the taxpayers that can, and will, legally be made to pick up the tab.

So they create big projects for their mates, who'll get fat bonuses, and as shareholders earn the profits for which they created the perfect environment to bloom. Socialising the costs and privatising the profits, as they say.

Well, but you'd have to be a cold-hearted, calculating actor for that. Some indeed are great actors, and some are not; the corruption droops from their faces as they sweat through public performances. The actors that have it worked out pull on their poker faces, always with a smile so the public always sees that nice guy, while instructing others to do the dirty political jobs, as we saw in the New Zealand tragicomedy called the 2014 elections. It went horribly wrong for the opposition of the National business party for many reasons. One main factor was the lack of a good director of the show. Mr Kim Dotcom should have stayed miles away from it, directing it like a chess player instead of posing in front of the audiences.

The National Party, on the other hand, was playing the game just like their American mates, well-controlled, well-acted, and played out their cards for a well-prepared audience that heard what they wanted to hear, which was not the Truth.

The Truth is something for special people, like the financial engineers on Wall Street trying to find the mechanisms that make the financially corruptible world roll in any direction. The Truth is that markets flow because of many different mechanisms, on different levels, from different directions, even in different dimensions.

Most people do not know, they do not understand and what is even more dramatic is that these people do not care to understand. Anything to keep the illusions in their minds intact. Many people don't want to hear the Truth. They just want constant reassurance that what they believe is the Truth.

The brainwash of "believing" is at at the core of the global problem. People say "you have to believe in something" as to confirm their own beliefs. Once you start believing, they can make you believe anything and everything. Hence the bought media, the organised religions, the fashions and the illusion we call "democracy".

There is no democracy in this corrupted world, but we want to believe it is a democracy just to soothe our minds, so we can continue the mind numbing entertainment we're so "deeply" involved in, so we can believe that all we did was good for our children, so we can all become one happy family of zombies.

Truth is, we don't want to hear it.

What would happen if we'd really want to know and understand the Truth? What would need to happen for us, for the people to be willing and capable, to know and understand the Truth? If you choose to believe, it means that you do not know and even worse, you do not understand. Because if you'd know, if you'd understand, you'd say "I know", or "I understand", instead of saying "I believe".

So, "believing" has become a global problem. It has become the basis on which marketing and propaganda are based. Assumptions rather than facts, wants rather than needs, lies rather than truths. Sometimes it is fun to watch what trickery they pull out of the hat, but it becomes dramatic, or even tragic, to see with what trickery they can get away with. "They", the beings in governments, acting as governments, the corporate lawyers, lobbyists, the shareholders, the kings and queens of the make-believe-land we call our modern world. The 1%, as we call them, composed of a core representing a mere 0.000001% of the world's population, with large circles of profiteers around them, growing like a cancer, with tentacles into the many layers of our global societies.

We prefer the fairy tales of kings and queens over the bitter truth that their amassed financial fortunes are not of a divine quality, but more that of criminals, murderers, corruption and thievery.

The legal power we believe they have also is based on illusions. Over time we have come to believe that every law they created for themselves is justified in its legality. Nothing could be further from the Truth... Imagine, what would you do if you were a criminal?

What would you do if you learned over time the workings of manipulations on different levels of people, human beings? What would you do if you were of a species that learned over thousands, millions of years, endless time, the workings of manipulations for a simple species called humans? What would you do if you found a growing opposition from within the humans, a growing awareness of what is, what is not, what could be, and what could have been?

Would you lay war on them? Would you legalise war on them? Would you legalise terror on them and use manipulative marketing/propaganda trickery to make it seem the opposite? Would you? I bet you would, if you were one of them.

So it is us vs. them. Rich vs. poor? Big vs. small? White vs. black? Christians vs. muslims? Men vs. women?

All of it, and none of it. At the core of it, I'd simplify it by saying Corrupt vs. the Rest. In every group, in every layer, we have good people and bad people. We all choose what to do in the circumstances we call life. There's always a choice. Some people choose to be corrupt, others are without realising it, and some choose to not be corrupt.

For corruption you only need two things. One is a corruptible system (Check), and two, corruptible people (Check). For corruption to become a legal part of a society, you only need corruptible people in your governments... Check!

The problem is, there isn't a problem, we've allowed them to create the perfect corruptible world for themselves. And we believe that, because it is all legalised, it must be OK, it must be justified.

Hell no, it is not justified. Not in a million years, not even in eternity. There is no justification for stealing from universal prosperity. There is no justification for keeping this place we call Earth from being the "Heaven on Earth" it could be for all. For all and not just for a few cold-hearted beings that put each other in legalised control positions, while living the decadent lives of fairy-tale kings and queens.

There is no justification for all of that. We need to find a cure for Earth for the cancer that is still growing.

"Inside Job"

As it just happened to be, a few days before watching "Inside Job", 2010, about the global financial crisis of 2008, I finished reading "The Quants" by Scott Patterson. Fascinating complementary perspectives on the same global problem.

"Just before their collapse these banks were given AA ratings...", during a congressional hearing the S&P managers and other credit rating institutions would just state that their ratings are "just an opinion". This was to mask that their ratings were bought, they had a choice to publish ratings as to please bankers, financial managers, financial engineers and receive millions of dollars for that, or simply get nothing. Of course the well weathered participants in the financial industry, the multi-million-dollar bonus managers know and knew very well how to interpret those ratings, but it's the general public, the provider of the bulk of financial profits, that gets the ratings veil over their eyes. "All is well, you can go to sleep again", so we can rob your society and nobody will be watching... And that same general public is the one that always pays for the bailouts, for the losses of any and all kinds, the taxes, the public debt that is created in their names and again, the multi-million-dollar bonuses for the mis-managers. Isn't that ironic? Or is it criminal?

Yes, we are dealing with international organised crime, and every shareholder nowadays is part of it. The issue is even more serious when it concerns a shareholder and a politician in one or any person in some kind of (public) position who should be way beyond the tiniest suspicion of corruption, or conflicts of interest. If credit ratings of this magnitude can be bought to mislead the public, then how about any other kind of report from any kind of referential institution that would have an image, a facade, of independent "expert opinion"?

There have been many attempts to regulate the corruptible bureaucratic financial world, but since politicians, especially in the USA, are legal participants, shareholders of that same corrupted world, they have multiple conflicts of interest; and being in the position to choose and still NOT legally regulate the financial markets against the criminal abuse that has been going on for ages, and is still going on in ever changing forms, may be just as bad as the greedy, cold-hearted money and global general wealth vultures themselves.

If we want this corrupted system to really change for the good of all mankind, we can not expect it to come from the pool of cold-blooded vultures that live on it.

When a (corporate) corrupted government legally controls spy agencies, then who will they be spying for?

When a (corporate) corrupted government legally creates new laws, then who will they be making laws for?

Note of Understanding

I do not believe.

You'd want me to believe in something, because "you have to believe in something"? Well, I don't and I won't. People who believe something can be made to believe anything. I choose to understand, I choose to feel the Essence, the Truth, I will not just believe it.

Believing is for organised religions, for propaganda, for marketing, for fairy tales, not for Truth. Believing is for those who are too lazy, too stupid to go and find the Truth. And when you find the Truth, consider it not the Truth, because beyond that Truth is another Truth, sometimes understandable, sometimes merely visible, sometimes not visible at all, that is, not yet. What we can not see, does that not exist? "I will believe it when I see it", that's not believing, that's knowing. But still not understanding.

The Truth is, there are many Truths, many dimensions, and many perspectives. The Truth is not just the Truth.

We have to transcend

We have to transcend above the current bureaucratic law system. Eventually we have to transcend far beyond the current bureaucratic law system. As it is now it is a reflection of the State of Mind "governing", controlling our societies. As it is now it is barbaric, it is evolved, transformed, adapted beyond its initial use, it is corruptible as hell and invites to be abused as such, by criminals. And who else will feel attracted to such a system? Organised crime, which exactly is what we are dealing with right now all around the globe. On multiple levels, from small crime to international organised crime. They have infiltrated every aspect of our businesses, corporations, councils and governments, and created the legal structures they need for their own personal advances.

The bureaucratic law system could have been an attempt to catch the Spirit of Justice into words, but the wordings have failed, and its interpretations have gone in any direction that money could buy. The Spirit of Justice is not captured in our laws, it is not even hidden in our laws.

Hiding behind multiple facades in organisations, both corporate and government, or even religious, criminal organisations are managed by cold-hearted control freaks, hoarding the illusion that we call money, while continuously taking away the financial instruments needed for the general public to prosper. Money that is taken out of our society to be hidden in offshore accounts or mountains of gold is non-productive, it does not help a society to prosper.

We have to transcend, but can not wait, or trust, for short-sighted control freaks to make this transition actually happen. They do not understand, as they are like reptiles, predatory, without the vision of warm-hearted, caring, intelligent beings. But because they are so cold-hearted, they are great actors; without caring about Truth, they will look you in the eyes while speaking sheer lies. They do not care, they can not care, they have no heart in their soulless bodies.

Who are they, if not caring, warm-hearted human beings? What are they?

The human mind consists of several main parts that each characterise different phases in evolution. There is the "reptilian brain", the Cerebellum, as opposed to the Cerebrum, that as an evolutionary part of the brain sits on top of the reptilian brain, which are connected with each other, just as the left and right hemisphere in the brains are connected, but different.

Einstein's well developed Corpus Callosum, the communicative highway between the left and right hemispheres, gave rise to him finding new understandings of this world, this existence. Different people have different bodies with different talents, different capabilities, the same as with the brain and the different parts it consists of. Researching the Corpus Callosum does not seem threatening to the current State of our Minds of our governments, but researching the quality of communication between Cerebrum and Cerebellum would.

If it would show, or only suggest to show, that in some

people the "reptile" Cerebellum is dominant over the more humane Cerebrum, it would certainly show that both criminals and politicians have similar hardware in their brains, meaning that cold-hearted behaviour is not just a choice, but is just the Modus Operandi that belongs to the mental system; politicians would hardly be interested to fund such research for that, and neither would greedy corporate managers...

So, we have to transcend, but are governed and controlled by beings whose interest it would be to change the system in the other direction than would be prosperous for the whole of humanity. How do you deal with a cancer? How do you deal with a cancer that aggressively spreads throughout the system? Can we cure cancer? And if we do, how can we make the organism healthy and strong enough to resist the next attack of a cancer?

As the human body is an organism consisting of many different parts, communicating, working together for the benefit of the whole, so is the entire human society, as a part of their existence on this planet we call Earth.

The insanity of wars, of wars for profit, of wars for control, of wars for religions, has nothing to do with the greater good for the whole, the One, or even for God. The insanity of tax systems, taking from the masses to give to the few, illustrate the ongoing intensification of control through illusions of lawfulness. The insanity of poisoning this world, its humans, its nature, its seas, its skies, its soils, for profits, for control. The insanity of money as a thing of intrinsic value, as an instrument for hoarding (financial) wealth, and then the illusion of monetary gold, a yellowish metal, expressed in another illusion called money... The insanity, the insanity, the insanity...

How did we get in such an insane world? We could have had "Heaven on Earth" for all, but instead have allowed the creation of multiple hells for many, and the hoarding of insane financial wealth and economic control, for just a few that do not care, that can not care, for that's what they are. They are not us, as they are not for us, and they do not care. They can not hide behind illusions of "knowing better", of controlling the world, manipulating the world to make it "better". You can not bomb the world into peace; it would become awfully quiet, but that's not peace. You can not bomb, starve or infect people into smaller numbers, or steal their means of existence to control them, without damaging, leaving deep scars in the Existence of Humanity. That is, if you would care.

There is a solution for everything, but it takes a far different kind of brain to come up with caring, considerate, respectful, loving, constructive, long-term solutions than the kinds of brains we have in our governments now.

As said before, for corruption you only need two things: A. a corruptible system, and B. corruptible people managing it.

We have to transcend beyond the current state, we have to.

They call themselves "Financial Engineers", they study at our public universities, but in reality strive to become "financial terrorists", and none of the corrupt politicians want to create legislation against them...

They were supposed to find Weapons of Mass Destruction in Iraq, but in November of 2002 a CIA front company called Bruster & Jennings intercepted a VX nerve gas shipment that was on its way across the border of Turkey into Iraq. That shipment should have been found after the invasion... That CIA front was led by Valerie Plame, who was subsequently outed as a CIA agent over a cover story that pointed to her husband's discrediting of Bush's Yellow Cake Uranium lie.

The meaning of Life?

Who wants to live forever? Why, and how? With what kind of eternal life would you be happy? What kind of eternal life would make sense? What kind of life would make sense at all? Is it the meaning of life that gives it its purpose?

There have been so many thoughts and writings about this issue, that I thought that everything that there is to say would have been said. Then I thought, maybe it's not about the answer, maybe it's about the question. When you do not ask the right question, you will not get the right answer. So, I went a step further towards the Essence, away from "just" Life; after all, Life as we know it only has meaning for us, humans, as such. What about Existence, the whole damn thing?

What is the meaning of Existence? What is the purpose of Existence?

I had no answer, so that question would lead me back to Life. What is the purpose of Life? And the answer that followed: the purpose of Life is to give meaning to Existence. It's not that Life was thrown into the mix to give meaning to Existence, it's only a logical connection, an interdependent relationship. But then, back to Existence. What is the logic behind it? And I don't mean the logic of physics, maths or any science for that matter. What is the logical purpose for Existence to exist at all?

Does it matter to be a good boy, or a bad girl? Or a good

girl, or a bad boy? Does it matter if "alien life" exists? Does it matter if Life is eternal or not? Does it matter if there is Life after death? Does it matter if there is Life after the Sun has run out of fuel? Does it matter if Existence is here or not? Does it matter if there is a God? Does it matter if there are Gods? Does it matter if we are Gods? Does it matter if Existence is eternal or not? Does it matter if this Existence is eternal or not?

What is the purpose of (this) Existence?

The only logical answer I could come up with was a horrible one: Existence has no purpose. No matter in what form, shape or dimensions, imaginable or unimaginable, Existence has no purpose. As you can imagine, this was not a satisfying answer. So, I came up with an answer that still haunts me, my mind still wrestles with it, my mind does not want to accept it. It feels like a cop-out, and yet, it feels logical: Existence is its own purpose. One may have to let this sink in for a few moments.

So, just like the process of coming to grips with the logic of endless time, accepting the logic of endless time, it is starting to grow on me, as if the room is being cleared to move to the next class, a higher class; Existence is its own purpose.

If I would repeat it often enough, would I start believing it? There is no logic in believing.

Believe.

Belief.

The belief industry

There is an entire belief industry which has three separated branches that sometimes intermingle: the religious belief industry, the commercial belief industry and the political belief industry.

The religious belief industry, or organised religion, has a long history, one that started ages before the industrial revolution. For the cause of my issue, it is not necessary to determine which religion was first, or which religion was best, or which religion was worst. I'd like to mention the Sumerian Tablets though. And even though they are dated at about 3000 BC, and describe stories that are similar to some found in the Bible, the simple logic of endless time tells us that there never has been a beginning, no beginning in Time, no beginning in Existence, no beginning in Lifeforms, as Life is not limited to what we think that Life is, or was. The Sumerian Tablets already refer to prehistoric ruins on a hill that make it difficult to grow crops. Just because we can not find visual proof of prehistoric cultures, or pre-prehistoric cultures, does that mean they weren't there? Is absence of proof, proof of absence?

What is left for us, is logic. The logic of reasoning is what helps me to accept truths that are not yet implemented in my life. When you have endless time, in a trial and error model, you can achieve anything just by testing, experimenting for the proper result. For individual humans, in Earthly life, the lifespan of the human body and mind are the limitations. For humanity the life span could be endless if it would not limit itself to time and place, as life on Earth seems limited to the life span of the sun. In a million years the sun won't provide us with life energy as it does now. In 500 billion years life may have left Earth altogether. As such, then what is the purpose of Life at all? What is the logic of living Life at all? Why would we be living at all? Why would we be existing at all?

For the human mind such questions can be troublesome. For most people the existence of endless time is hard to grasp, or even the existence of other realities than the 4D reality we are in on Earth. I remember struggling with the idea, and noticing over time that I was getting used to it, getting familiar with it, accepting it as a reality of this Existence. Like an athlete trains his or her body, I learned I can train my mind to go beyond where it was, to see and understand realities on and from a different plane, to travel from plane to plane.

And that is where organised religions come in, they close the mind, keep it entangled in a mind frame, a harness, a control system. Suggestions of fear or punishment on the one hand, and the suggestion of unconditional love on the other, it does not rhyme. Which loving father could or would punish any of his children with something like hell?

How can anyone be truly happy in something like Heaven, while knowing that a loved one, or many loved ones, or even anyone, would be in hell? Would you punish your children with something like hell because you love them?

There is no logic in this, but there is a purpose for such illusions: to control people. To make them behave as controlled individuals, in the way you want them to behave. To make them behave as a group, a herd, a flock, in the way you want to use them.

To make them behave as one, an entity of thoughtless minds, believing that what they do for their religion saves them from the punishment of hell. Selfish, full of fear, without understanding what Love really is, and yet believing that their understanding of what love is, is the truth. Because their religious interpreter, their leader, told them so.

I feel no hate, and I have no hate, against religious people. There can be a lot of beauty in a religion, but there also can be a lot of ugliness in a religion. One of the great lessons I learned from religion is to always choose the narrow gate, the hard road, instead of the easy way out, the cop-out, the convenient lie. Another one is that religions do not teach people what Love is. "Love thy neighbour like thyself"? Why not love everyone? Or is that the narrow gate, the tough road? While it would be so simple, and everyone could feel happy, safe, cared for, loved...

What is Love anyway? Is it to cause anyone pain or destroy their lives? Would a loving God approve of any such thing? Or is it that humans are made to believe that their God loves his creation so much that he likes it to be ruined instead of being enjoyed, shared and taken care of? Could I be more loving than the loving-God?

I don't think so, so what is the issue here?

Here we come back to the light-orb. One explanation of what the light-orb could be, to me, is a lifeform that captures the same soul (what ever that may be) that gives life to our human bodies, but in a different form, a different dimension maybe. I imagine it to be a basic lifeform, a very basic soul container, or maybe a very advanced one. No matter what, in that condition it will be able to do things we can not with our Earthly, human bodies. But, having learned from my architectural education, limitations are opportunities. I came to see that a soul on Earth, captured in a human body, will have to engage in opportunities such as problems, hardships, beauty, love, in a way that it could never experience in the form or reality of a light-orb. Our Existence on this Earth, in these dimensions, in these conditions, gives us unique learning and experiencing possibilities. In that way Earth is a place of learning, a place of experiencing, a place of adventure, a place of both heaven and hell.

Our existence on this globe could be like Heaven on Earth for each and everyone, but it is not.

Remember only just a little while ago, how organised religions accepted that Earth was not flat? For ages people believed the authorities of their organised religions to be right, so, for something so fundamental to be so horribly wrong, shouldn't that be a warning for other issues?

Why would a God who can have anything and everything need to collect gold, palaces, dressed up controllers who make rules for their flock just as it suits them? I think all these "houses of God" in fact are the opposite of what they present to be. All of this has nothing to do with Love. In fact, I think they are an insult to God, whatever, or whoever God may be, or not be.

The political belief industry

When you take an organised religion, and leave out the God factor, then what is left is the structure of controlling political propaganda. When you believe, you accept as Truth what you do not know to be true. Once religious organisations started to become control organisations, they already had become political organisations. At some point all religious organisations are, or have become political organisations, and nowadays it sometimes is hard to see if you're dealing with a political religious organisation, or with a religious political organisation. They seem to go back and forth, just like the fashion of the day, adapting to the marketing need of the day.

Politics has become the latest fashion for bureaucrats, no matter in business, religion or government. Political strategies like "dirty politics" have become the norm in a world full of organised crime. White-collar crime, blue-collar crime, so just having an expression, a label for it makes it (seem) normal?

The strategies of religious beliefs have become known in circles outside of organised religions, and as such also have been studied and even taught in Universities. "Political science", maybe there should be a law against it? But who would be in the position to make such a law?

In its early days politics was a job of honour, often even without pay, but with more or less significant influence. Royalty (whatever that may be) used to be heavily involved, and often would be dictating politics. Nowadays they are seemingly less involved, and maybe they need not be, because they have organised their daily affairs quite nicely around regulations and laws that guarantee them a nice way of luxurious living, and even are admired for it by the ones who give them the money to keep the illusions alive, plus a close circle of profiteers who will put effort in keeping the system as it is out of self-interest. Many people actually believe that our (modern) "royalty" is normal, as if it has always been there, in the endlessness of times. People believe those illusions, instead of knowing, comprehending, that most, if not all, "royalty" came into existence after a series of crimes, and that the creation of such illusions (of "royalty") shades, filters away the truths of (their) histories.

In modern politics we see the highest ranks in society, business and governments behaving more and more as if they are "royalty" with their privileged lives. When I see the decadence in which modern presidents entourage themselves, I immediately think of the history lessons about Louis XIV, about the Old Romans, how decadence comes before the fall. And yet, people still believe all of this is normal, even logical.

When I grew up in the Netherlands, as a kid, I saw politics and politicians as very special, honourable bureaucrats, who all would defend the special interests of the groups they represented. I thought this was normal, because I grew up as such, and everyone seemed to accept it as such.

Now that I live in New Zealand, as an adult, I see a very

different kind of politics. I see immature men, and women behaving like immature men, without the integrity I used to see in politicians. I see patterns in international politics, similar to organised crime, but then so deeply infiltrated, that, similar to what was the case with religion and politics, it is hard to see what exactly is what. Where does the organised crime become politics, and vice versa? When is a politician corrupt? When is a politician part of (global) organised crime? How come we see the same (criminal, corrupt) patterns in politics appearing in all "westernised" countries, around the world?

When did it become normal to mix politics with religion, politics with business, or even politics with sport and other entertainment?

I find it hard to accept that people believe the lies politicians are telling us and still accept them as reliable managers of our societies. Why would you choose, for such an important job, the kind of people who are the exact opposite of what you would need for such a position? The only reason that such a situation can exist is because we all believe(d) that the bureaucratic law system represents Justice.

There can be no Justice in a corruptible legal system that is managed by corruptible career bureaucrats. It's only a matter of time until such a system is corrupted and abused for private and organised crime interests. The system is managed by the same people who create the laws that "legally" immunise them against prosecution for the crimes they committed, and plan to commit in the future. The kind of people who are attracted to such a system are cold-hearted, selfish, immature beings, most often poorly educated, while the kind of people we'd need for a healthy government would be warm-hearted, socially aware and caring, mature and well-educated. It's logical that the selfish, cold-hearted group will use and abuse the system they created for their own benefit, no matter the cost to society.

As long as people believe that bureaucratic law equals Justice, we'll have these (career) bureaucrats misleading the way, and greedy corporate managers, their lobbyists and their share holders love (to keep) it that way. As such, the judicial belief industry, as a part of the political belief industry, is at the core of the problem of our societies.

The commercial belief industry

I see marketing as commercial propaganda and propaganda as political marketing, but of course that's only half the story. Before all was the religious belief industry, and there was and still is religious marketing and religious propaganda, at all different levels, stages, angles of the same game. And that game has won such an interest in those who wish to manipulate people, markets, that an entire industry erupted with experts of various kinds of illusory trades.

Labels, symbols, logos, brands and trademarks; where does propaganda begin, or marketing end?

Remember those sneaky split-second visual frames in movies, for commercial (subliminal) purposes? Or the satisfied smoking hero, no matter after an adventurous episode in the jungle, on the battle field or in bed?

I remember the futuristic paintings of hovering cars, the promises of 20-hour working weeks and lots of healthy, clean, social leisure time. We'd all be so happy together while the robots would do all the hard work for us. Helas we already had forgotten about Nikola Tesla and his ideas of free energy in the beginning of the 20th century. You can't hang a meter on free energy, so our greedy, cold-hearted corporate and financial business leaders put an end to that dream.

When Edward Bernays stepped up to the stage, marketing, in the form of Public Relations, was very actively promoted and researched. The wizards of P.R. even created illusions around themselves, the marketing of the belief industry, as if all they said was new, ignoring that religious marketing was already many ages old. Political marketing, however, never before had taken such a vast form. And to make it even less transparent, where did commercial propaganda come in? Or how could propaganda and marketing even become one?

The complex mix that marketing and propaganda have become, with both having their tangles in Edward Bernays's Public Relations, moved to something that we'll call "dirty politics". It happened when cold-hearted, greedy men came in positions of political power so they could manipulate entire societies in ways that would further their private commercial interests: profits and greed. As shareholders and as lawmakers and policymakers their lack of comprehension of what makes life matter, or what matters in life, created a society that came to believe that greed and its accompanying abuse of power are normal.

The news media have been bought, and sold, to end up as an advertising apparatus that publishes the news that is in the interest of its owners and advertisers; big money, of all sorts.

Do not expect a critical article about vaccines when the vaccine industry buys large advertising spaces.

Do not expect a critical article about clean rivers being polluted by dairy effluent when the dairy industry invests significantly in advertising.

Do not expect a critical article about the military when defence (government and/or industry) buys entire pages for advertising.

Money talks in marketing land. People sell their soul when they believe it's the only way they can survive. There's too much believing and too little comprehension. Sure, you can comprehend the ins and outs of publishing, marketing, public relations (peacetime propaganda), but where does that get you when it makes you blind for anything that is beyond that shallow scope?

The arrogance of propaganda and marketing relies on the lack of proper education and information for the people, that's how I see it. The idea of Edward Bernays that the American public needed to be "guided from above" still forms the basic belief structure from which American politics (government, business and religion) are being managed. If, however, the American public would have been properly educated and informed, there would be no need for such guidance it would become natural to make wise choices.

But, then again, those who make the legal rules now also are the ones who do not want the public to be properly educated and informed. The system, therefore, is corrupted to the bone.

For corruption you only need a corruptible (legal) system, and corruptible people managing it. Political marketing and commercial propaganda became one when governments got infiltrated by agents, lobbyists and shareholders of corporations with huge cold-hearted commercial interests.

From my short history in the medical pharmaceutical industry I remember the selfish, cold-hearted manipulations of marketing bureaucrats, who, very similarly to government bureaucrats, have a talent to destroy the things that are relevant to life.

"Bureaucrats take the life out of anything, and everything they can lay their hands on".

The system is out of control; the bureaucratic lawmakers create self-serving laws and the bureaucratic overhead becomes heavier and heavier. It grows like a cancer that eats, destroys anything and everything in its way. It's only a matter of time until it collapses, very similarly to the corruptible financial systems that have been installed all around the globe. The burden becomes heavier and heavier. And in the meantime the global banking organised crime syndicate has harvested the interest from all created debt and wars, and invested it in the privatised national assets that corrupt politicians were willing to sell, to counter all the debt, as they said.

Are the next Nuremberg trials set yet? It's about time.

The beauty of the Truth, the beauty of Truths, in any and all forms and dimensions. The beauty of all Truths.

Bureaucracy

The issues with bureaucrats are old ones, but then again relatively new too. Since when did we have bureaucrats? Why do we have bureaucrats? Is there a way to have less or no bureaucrats?

Bureaucrats are a layer in our society that is growing thicker and thicker; they deal with numbers, they register, make rules or even laws. And then they defend or attack those rules and laws. All at a price; which is one of my main issues with bureaucrats, bureaucrats are not productive, in the sense that they would create something tangible, or essential for society as a whole.

Career bureaucrats create the layers and step ladders they need for their own careers, and fill the lower layers with lower bureaucrats to form the mass they need to be able to stand on, to step upon, to step up. From high above, there's a segment, a special layer, filled with the top bureaucrats who piss down on the rest below, their very own trickle down effect. They create the corporate and government rules to give themselves huge bonuses, while referring to each other as "the market price", a continuous, neverending suggestive, upward spiral. And they made us all believe this is normal. Clearly the illusion works, as the lower ranks see the ladder, and fight each other for one step up, and start behaving in the same way that they despised from their lower positions. The view from the top of the career bureaucrat ladder, as I imagine, is a very cold one, very distant, disconnected, selfish and one of show, theatre, illusion and propaganda. Orwell's "1984" comes to mind, but from a contemporary perspective it has become more commercialised, where propaganda meets marketing, where control power and financial power become the same distant, cold-hearted career goals for career bureaucrats, in both government and business positions and just as easily they hop from one side to the other, carefully creating the theatrical illusion that the two are still miles apart and serve different interests. In the ages of royal control, the royal lobbyists manipulated politics, or even took a seat in governments, and nowadays corporate lobbyists, with immense budgets, do the same thing, and indeed take seats in our governments, create the legislations they need for their corporate interests, and get away with it, because it's all "legal". And with royalty becoming shareholders, we're back at the beginning, or even worse, a downward spiral?

In essence bureaucracy is the realm of control freaks; in their minds there is a fear of losing control, which leads to an absence of humanity, the human factor. First they switch it on, they switch it off, on and off, until a moment where the off position becomes more or less permanent, because lack of some kind of humanity fits best with being a bureaucrat. Cold-hearted bureaucracy means less moral issues to deal with, better bureaucratic productivity, better control, and less humanity.

Most clearly, I think, this shows in everything related to art. When boring bureaucrats start to write regulations for any kind of art, they restrict the creative extent in which any form of art could travel or evolve. Concepts of decency, political correctness or mere personal preferences have proven forms of control that stamp out creative expressions that fall out of line with bureaucratic regulations. In its more extreme forms we can refer to dictatorships, fascist regimes, communist party censorship and any variations thereof.

In the food industry, corrupt regulations dictate the "correct" size and shape of produce, labels confirm or ignore its origins (country and/or GMO), or the amount of pesticides that can be used. Anything that can be abused for some kind of profit will be abused, because it's what the system allows for. Control bureaucrats now want to restrict home gardening, even when a few decades earlier it was the other way around, when government would stimulate people to grow their own food.

In medicine rigid regulations make machines out of doctors and doctors turn into cold profit-driven money makers, as the system drives out the humane factor. In hospitals nowadays there is more (control) management then there are doctors, while bureaucratic managers dictate the rules of engagement. They do not care, they do not understand and they do not understand that they do not care and they do not care that they do not understand what a hospital could really be. Like all career bureaucrats they see the system (hospital) as an instrument for their own careers instead as the other way around. In fact, this kind of thinking spreads like a disease, and meanwhile they keep pushing the agenda of the pharmaceutical industries, including the vaccine industries. Yes, control bureaucrats take the life out of anything and everything they can lay their hands on.

To make matters worse, it's also in (the) education (industry). Corrupt privatisations as usual and dictatorship of the curriculum as to make sure that students do not learn too much so they will not become a threat to the corrupt system; but, then again, learn enough to become obedient tax- and work slaves for the industries that lobby our governments.

Last but not least, the law system. Why do we accept laws that are made by incomplete human beings? Why do we let immature beings dictate our lives, our societies? The corruptible bureaucratic law system is invented as a service, as a protective illusion, for the people who profit from it. It has its roots in the ancient past and over the years served the different elites of the specific eras.

Since when do we have bureaucrats?

Where did this all start?
Was it the churches (organised religions)?
Was it the kings (feudalism)?
Was it the Egyptian pharaohs?
Was it the Sumerians?
Was it the Neanderthals?

Somewhere, somehow we suddenly had bureaucrats.

It was not like someone, somewhere had an idea of becoming a bureaucrat, even though the word did not yet exist, the bureaucrat was created out of a need. Whose need? The need of a small group of people who had the power to regulate, dictate, control and own what others could not. And the funny thing is, bureaucracy gave them even more power; an illusion of power, though, because once rules for people were written down, people believed that the written word of bureaucratic law was true and represented Justice, because the written word said so.

While the word "bureaucracy" has its origins in 18th century France, where Jacques Claude Marie Vincent de Gournay referred to a societal illness he called "bureaumania", the phenomenon has its origins far deeper down the line.

The oldest forms of bureaucracy are found in Sumer, ca. 3500 BC. Clay tablets were used to record and direct where the harvests would go. This seems relatively harmless compared to the Romans and their deeply organised administrative (control) districts, which were even outdone by their successor, the Byzantine Empire. On the other side of the world, under the Han dynasty, another empire of bureaucratic control evolved, was reformed, but continued until the beginning of the 20th century, deeply affecting the way the Chinese people and their society still act today. When people are deeply controlled for many generations it leaves its rigid traces behind, which in the modern world of intercontinental travel and investments quite often creates social and cultural irritations. We'll have to see how the (near) future develops, something has to give.

What I see happening in the Western world is the creation of controlled societies that greatly resemble the Chinese model of bureaucratic control, but then as a service to established corporate interests, which is the same evolution as happened in China, but then the other way around, with the same end result:

corporations dictating the bureaucratic controllers, a proven model for organised corruption.

Under systemic capitalistic abuse, Orwell's "1984" became a model for multinational corporate control. Corporate bureaucrats and government bureaucrats have become each other's complementary control force.

I remember the first time I clearly understood organised corruption was when I noticed the same bureaucrat working one moment for the government, and the next moment for Carlyle, and back; the revolving door phenomenon. One year they'd work in government, preparing and creating specific legislations, and the next year they'd go back to business, to harvest the legalised fruits. To sum it up into one simple statement, I do not think there is one country more deeply corrupted than the USA, and then we haven't even mentioned yet the American financial system, with its private Federal Reserve Bank.

Can there be an end to all of this? One way or the other there has to be an end to this, in a good way, or in a bad way. Those who are responsible for creating the economic illusions, for greed and control, can either come to their senses, become caring, responsible humans, and stop the war zones of all kinds, to make this world, this Existence, prosperous and healthy again; or there will inevitably be a moral collapse that will evaporate any kind of true happiness, for each and everyone. But then, the problem is that the creators, the organisers of this (global) mess, would not know what they'd be missing, what true happiness would look like, as their understanding of what happiness is, is limited to their narrow, closed minds.

Yes, we do have a problem here; the ones who should be changing are the ones who legally pull the strings of the system we live in, a system that serves the bureaucrats, and they do not want to change that, and neither do the corrupt "elites" who they serve.

Is there a way to have less or no bureaucrats? Assuming that bureaucrats primarily serve the system and only secondarily the citizens in the system, it seems that, in order to have less bureaucrats, we'd not just have to alter the system, but entirely remove it.

Who wants to do that? Not the bureaucrats... In a different system, that puts responsibilities with the citizens, the citizens need to be mature enough to take that responsibility. They need to be well-educated, and well-informed, and then a natural joy in taking responsibilities will emerge.

Do you believe in Bureaucracy, does one have to believe in Bureaucracy? Over the course of many years I learned to see Bureaucracy as a religion; you have to believe in it to accept it as being just. If one can not imagine a world without tax, or without money, surely it will become impossible to imagine a world without bureaucracy? Surely some bureaucracy may always remain, as to serve people though, not to serve the system itself.

The core, the backbone, the heart, the essence.

The Bureaucratic Law system is based on belief, the Moral Justice system is based on knowing and understanding. With so many different bureaucratic law systems, with ever-increasing mass of bureaucratic control and corruption, it should've become clear by now that it is a road to hell. Moral Justice, as I imagine it, is a simple description of what "Respect", "Freedom", "Trust" and "Love" are, how they relate to each other and form the Essence of our Existence, here, now, and for the future.

Everything that we do can be held against those four perspectives, to be valued and judged. However, it is a system of depth, of multiple dimensions, instead of flat bureaucratic rules, meaning we'd need a different kind of judges, judges who are beyond the set of flat bureaucratic rules, who truly understand the meaning of the words Respect, Freedom, Trust and Love. We need a different system, and a different management, a different kind of people.

The current bureaucratic law systems all are variations of one and the same rigid control system. Because of this rigidity the interpretations can be made in any direction with the consequence that the system can be abused in any direction. With a justice system that is based on morality rather then rigid rules, there is flexibility, relativity, fluidity that adapts in any direction, fitting each case into its own parameters. Morality in law is a focus on core properties, the essence, instead of focusing on the weaknesses of the words.

In a system of Moral Justice each case can be judged by asking the same three questions:

How does it conflict with the law of Respect?
How does it conflict with the law of Freedom?
How does it conflict with the law of Trust?

And the final, backup question, that completes the matter:
How does it conflict with the law of Love?

It will be clear that such questions in a Court of Law require a specific kind of judges, judges who truly understand the meaning of these words and the consequences they hold for a prosperous, healthy, mature and caring (global) society that represents both each individual and each group, larger and smaller, local, national and international. I say "global" and "international", because I want institutions like the United Nations or the International Criminal Court in The Hague to be based on these same principles, as there can not be Justice when (an illusion of) Justice is created by the size of one's budget.

This is a threat to a huge, fat and decadent layer of law professionals and shareholders, as they are advisers, lobbyists, profiteers of a self-serving system that generates huge amounts of money, directly and indirectly. Directly for the professionals and indirectly by the corruption from within the system they manage and control.

For a world to have real Justice, to be healthy, prosperous, mature and caring, we also need a different education and information system, all away from corporate (financial) interests.

Envision the world in 500 years. Do we want it to be a world that is controlled by the same corruption we have now, or do you see a world with well-educated, well-informed, caring people, who enjoy taking responsibilities and enjoy a very small judicial system? Small, because there is no need for a large judicial system, because people are well-educated, well-informed, and learned to enjoy taking responsibility for their choices; their actions and their inactions.

Control conflicts with "learning to let go"

The path to maturity is followed by the journey to wisdom. One of the obstacles is learning to let go. You can see this at a personal level, by learning to let go of traditions that serve no purpose, by learning to let go of needs that we believed were essential, by learning to let go of beliefs that have no fundamental truths in them. As an individual it becomes a direct reflection on your reality, but "learning to let go" as an entire community, as an entire society, will have an even stronger effect, as the individual effects will potentiate each other. Entire societies will be able to change quickly, grow towards wisdom, solve and avoid conflicts, a natural, not restrictive form of control.

What is it that the media write about nowadays?

It's been a process, a well-organised process, a plan. Journalism changed from journalism to entertainment, infotainment, propaganda, marketing. In New Zealand we saw, within a few years, the total destruction of public television, of independent reporting, to amusement shows, propaganda heads, readily willing to sell their souls to the corporate message.

Sports, the sports industry, the gambling industry, snacks and drinks, sportswear, sportsgear, an entire industry revolving around an illusion of activity, health and wealth.

Bright colours, happy people, athletic bodies, the modern arena, the "panem et circenses" of the 20th and 21st centuries. Just like 2000 years ago, the modern gladiators live in luxury, the entertainment nonsense is celebrated with illusions of greatness, of heroic proportions even, which in essence doesn't make a difference between the distance of 2000 years.

In a sane world, would anyone be knighted for playing with balls, scoring points in a game that brings the organisers millions, or even billions?

In a sane world, would we watch in awe how actors are celebrated by the same industry that makes millions, even billions from sheer entertainment?

Maybe indeed it's quite an achievement to generate billions of dollars by entertaining people. How did so many people come to believe in the world of industrial entertainment, industrial show, industrial gambling, industrial marketing. Just like a religion, organised, industrialised illusions, or "mind fuck" as Randy Pausch would have said.

But, you have to believe in something, right?

There is no logic in believing. People who believe one thing can be made to believe anything. So therefore I prefer to know and understand, to comprehend, to use a less tarnished word than "under-standing". Because comprehending the Essence of a matter is not like standing under something, it is more like hovering over the matter.

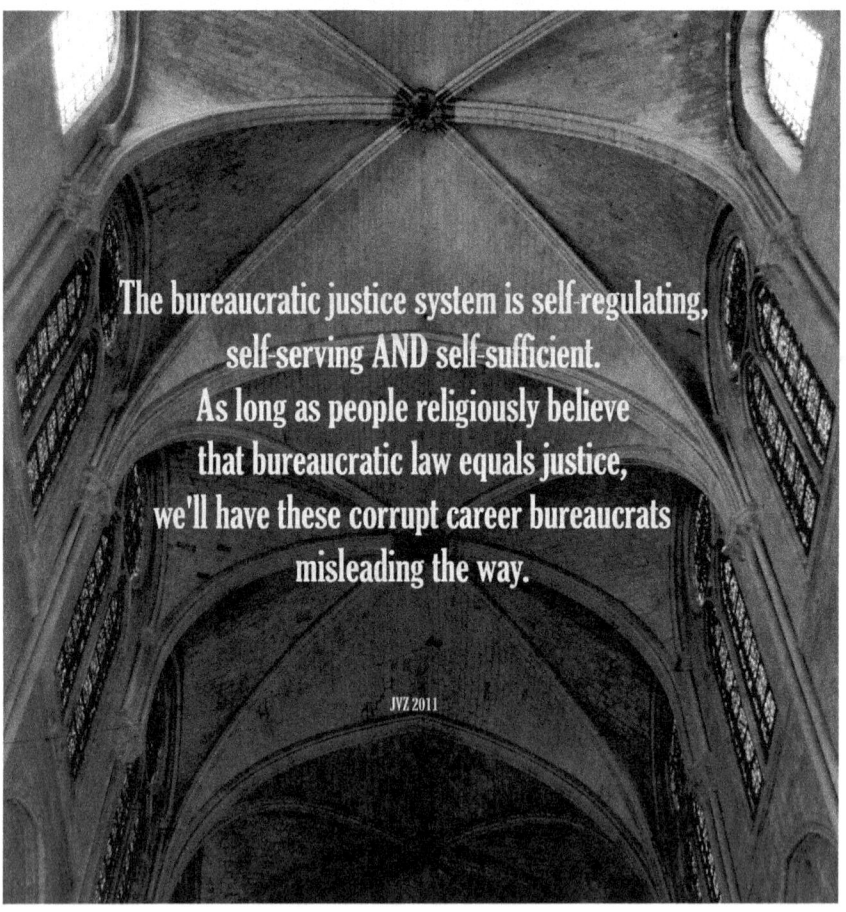

Become who you are

From a very different perspective, but with similar consequences: first become who you are, and then become who you can be.

The initial model had a square with a cross in it, which is now represented by the baseball bats. The shape was to resemble a pyramid, with another upside-down pyramid on top of it. It would represent a process that in time culminates into a point and then flips over on the other side. To become who you are was a process where slowly in time a concentration, an increased form of density would be formed and on top of that process a new world would open, and ever-widening possibilities would present themselves.

Later I saw this process more as the curves of the baseballs, where the moment of being who you are, transforming into becoming who you can be would be more of a flow into the higher state of change, of growth.

The first would be a sudden moment of awakening, the second would be a natural flow into awakening. Maybe the Truth is a mix of the two; I'm still not sure about it. Anyway, the point of it all is that when you're young your mind gets filled with a lot of baggage, often garbage, that keeps you from becoming who you really are. It keeps you from the potential being you could be. You will notice that when you become who you are, a new world opens, and widens as you move along.

Most people will never come to fulfil the first stage, becoming who they really are. The world is more, or "Die Welt ist mehr" as I wrote in my poem Zeistgeist, in 1997. I didn't know then what I know now, but I saw the opening, and could peek through.

FIVE SECONDS

If I wa

s God.

If I was God

(I sent this article in as a submission on the TED forum in 2012, and after being a respected member of the TED community for several years, consequently was kicked out of the TED community and all my other posts were deleted. As one may expect my views towards TED had changed accordingly.)

If I was God, I would not care about any organised religion claiming to represent the word of God. If I was God, I would not care about any organised religion building "houses of God". If I was God, I would not care about any organisation claiming to do anything "in the name of God".

What is this arrogance, this ignorance in human beings, making them believe rather than trying to really understand? Making themselves vulnerable to manipulations and propaganda?

Why would any God, of omnipresence, no matter what time, what place, what dimension, care about human beings worshipping God?

Why don't they understand that time never had a beginning? That existence never had a beginning? That human existence only is a small glimpse of reality? That human reality only is a small glimpse of existence?

Why would any God not care about humans seeking to understand (more of) the truth of existence, while out of love giving them the opportunities to understand freedom, respect and trust, so they can learn and experience what love really is?

Why would any God, from this unlimited existence, in any direction, in any dimension, care about a book of religious stories, that does not explain the essence of existence? Because if it would explain and help understanding this essence, it would make people make different choices than they do now.

People choose to be ignorant, people choose to be indifferent, people choose to be arrogant, people choose to not care.

Imagine, time never had a beginning, therefore existence never had a beginning. This means that anything is possible, even what we think is impossible. Time and space are one, but they also exist separately. Existence is One, but within this One existence there are also separate realities. You can look down on human dimensions, to see what is going on, but you can not see what is going on above the level of the human perspective. Dimensions unimaginable for most humans exist at the same time as our human existence. Just because humans can not see them does not mean that they do not exist.

Before the existence of the microscope did bacteria exist, or did they come into existence because of the microscope?

If I was God I would not interfere in human existence, as an expression of love for freedom, for respect, for trust. But, if I was God, looking at Earth, seeing all the violence, all the destruction, all the manifestations of organised hate, I would come to a point where enough is enough. Existence on Earth could be what Heaven would be like; in fact, existence on Earth, from a multi-dimensional point of view, is Heaven. For the sake of love, for the sake of understanding love for existence, our lives on Earth are an expression of freedom, of respect and trust. We have been given the opportunities to experience on Earth what we could not experience in this form anywhere else.

But, some human beings behave like a cancer, ruining the place for the rest of us. They are a shame in the face of the essence of our existence. So, if I was God, I would remove this cancer, in the name of love; clean up the place, from the inside out, and from the outside in. It is time to clean up this place, and with the help of God, the best place to look for this God in this existence is simply in your heart.

17-09-2015

Two days ago I heard that my mother's health had dropped significantly. We already had heard about her cancer about a month ago, but suddenly it went for the worse.

A few weeks ago she had discussed euthanasia with her physician; however, in the Netherlands euthanasia is in the hands of the bureaucrats. The bureaucrats found a way, constructed around strict rules. To avoid the problem people are put in a coma, and simply left to die; no food, no drink, just die. A horrible, slow way to die, but in the way of the bureaucrats, a legal way, so it's all good...

Now, suddenly my mother seemed to have had a lack of oxygen, which caused some damage to her brain, and now, suddenly, the way to a more humane way to die is closed, because, according to the rules, she has to be able to be fully aware when she gives her consent to the doctor who'd give her the final intravenous injection. So, there you go, the bureaucratic control system even manages to ruin the last moments of a painful, deteriorating life.

Life is not about "Justice". There is no justice in a life, that ends with cancer, there is no justice in a deteriorating life, that is worsening dramatically, there is no justice in a life that is made to suffer even more because of bureaucratic rules. Since when do bureaucrats understand what life is? So why are we allowing them to make the rules for our lives? Life is not about Justice, so don't waste it running after that illusion.

Life is not about a "feel good" factor, life is not what we've been made to believe it is. Please let us stop allowing those "decent" bureaucrats and their corruptible bureaucratic law system to control our lives, our Existence, or even our deaths.

15-10-2015

My mother died about two weeks ago, in her sleep. She seemed to have recovered somewhat, but on her birthday it got worse again. Where I live, on the other side of the globe, according to Maori oratory, there is a very elegant white bird, the Kotuku, that is said to be a messenger from the afterworld. During the last few years, every summer a Kotuku came to the wetlands in front of our house; a very rare sight, as there are only 150-200 Kotuku in New Zealand. As such "as rare as a Kotuku" is often used as a reference to how special or beautiful something or someone is.

On the day after my mother's birthday I suddenly saw two Kotuku in front of my house, in a treetop. This had never been seen before, I heard from locals; just the one Kotuku already was a rare occasion. The two stayed in front of the house all morning, were gone fishing for a moment and came back to that same tree, close to my house. After a while I noticed one of the two was gone, when the other flew up to the closest tree to my house, and from the treetop looked around for a while, during sunset.

The next day they both were gone, and I haven't seen either of them after that day.

Two days later I heard that my mother had died during the very moments that the two Kotuku sat in front of my house, and I did remember asking myself if my mother had passed away when the two Kotuku sat there so elegantly and peacefully.

I don't know, and I don't just believe anything. But, it looked and felt beautiful.

Dimensions, life, or existence, after death?

Imagine being colour blind, and someone describing a rainbow of colours to you. Or imagine being deaf, and someone explaining Beethoven's 9th Symphony.

You can look down from a higher dimension, but you can

not just look up into a higher dimension. But, a being (in no matter what form) from a higher dimension can come down to show itself in the reality, and within the properties, of that lower dimension.

And that is what I think happened with the orb. I imagine the vision of the orb to be one of joy, seeing a world that, by its specific limitations, becomes more beautiful. A local beauty, fixed to this time and place, and these dimensions. Imagine the amount of local beauties for the dimensional traveller. Imagine an infinite world, an infinite existence, multiple dimensions, and then a holiday of limited dimensions on Earth, with all of its unique properties, qualities, possibilities, limitations, opportunities.

The von Neumann probe

There is a phenomenon called the von Neumann probe, which refers to a "time machine", a googling apparatus, thing, that may be remote-controlled, in our time and space, from a different time (the future), and/or a different dimension. The way I experienced the orb was like a "living machine". It could be a "soul pod", the basic form of (a) being, independently thinking, operating, "feeling", or just with a straightforward mission, like a living robot?

From the limitations of life on Earth come unique opportunities, that are the consequence of this existence, these dimensions, this specific moment in time and space. "Feeling", or even the concept of "Love" may therefore be unique to our "here and now". Just as we tend to project our personal feelings, interpretations, on to other people, we also tend to see Existence from our projecting minds, as to make sense of it, to be able to grasp it, or to avoid the confrontation with a distant reality.

Did the orb communicate?

Some people asked me that, and I had to say that it didn't, as this was my first impression. But after some time I asked myself, what would be the purpose of this close encounter if there had not been any communication? And then it became clear to me that it might have been the smartest way to handle the situation; it communicated by simply showing itself, nothing more, and nothing less. If it had done more, it could have ruined the encounter, it could have been too much, in every sense.

By keeping it small and simple, it stayed relatively comprehensible, no matter how incomprehensible it seemed, or was. But by adding a new appearance that was uniquely different from all other light orb videos and pictures, it showed something very special was going on. And what it was, we still have to find out, maybe it's "just" the fact that I was the right person to do "the job", what ever that may mean. As an intelligent person, with my specific background I could imagine that that would make sense, without vanity or pride. OK, a bit of pride I do feel about this unique experience, it's however a mixture of happiness and worry, from seeing and comprehending this reality in a way that most people can not, for the simple fact that they did not see it. So they'd just have to believe it?

Never just believe, make sure you know, and comprehend, with logic, and your heart. So, no, don't just believe what I said, because then anyone could come along and make false statements, that even could seem more appealing, and by just believing he, or she, could lead you astray, like a Pied Piper. The Truth, the Essence, is not in other people or beings. The Truth, in these dimensions, in this reality, is in you.

Flat Earth, round Earth?

In an infinite world, an infinite space, the only way to naturally, logically and optimally form and contain a reality like a world, is a spherical shape.

In a theory of flat Earth, where would it be grounded, where would be Ground Zero, where would it start, what would be the point, what would be the logic? Of course, the logic of Existence relates to the dimensions that one grew up with, the dimension one accepted as being normal, the dimensions one has come to grips with. Beyond those dimensions, the logic that belongs to those dimensions becomes untouchable for the limited human mind.

So, would a flat Earth with a base in endless space and time be logical in distant dimensions?

Would the magic of endless space and time provide a magical basis for a flat Earth? If so, why hasn't anyone seen it? Have we finally arrived at the real Fermi paradox then? If flat Earth is real, why haven't we seen pictures from its side yet?

So, for practical reasons, I simply refer to my flights around the world, at 30,000-40,000 feet, where I noticed that the horizons around me always stayed at the same visual distance, which is proof of a round Earth, or a gigantic projection in my head, specifically made for me. Then this entire reality would be a projection, specifically for me, with or without interaction with others like or not like me. Whether or not this reality is a projection, a creation in or by my mind, it doesn't matter for the consequences, it doesn't change the logics of causes and effects, the realities in these dimensions, this Existence. The Matrix is real, but then again, is our reality also?

When you close one world, reality or dimension, another one opens. The possibilities are endless.

Reality

When I was taking a shower this morning, I held up my hand and saw how water accumulated in it. I thought about the amount of space between atoms, and how this water did not seem to seep through me, but when I turned my hand gravitational force pulled the water to the floor.

I thought about the movie "The Matrix", where the Merovingian's tale of cause and effect is visualised as in 4D, showing a hollow computer wire model, which is the basic visual structure that is needed to show the effect, while reflecting on one of the dimensions of the Matrix itself. Seeing that, I realised that, with a different kind of eyes, my reality would be different from what I perceive it to be now. A blind person sees with his/her ears, the nose, the touch and maybe another sense of awareness that we have not yet described a specific receiver for. What if I had eyes that would see in a different dimension, with different receptors, and I would only see the structures beyond the surface? My reality would be quite different. For instance, maybe I would see through the hollow spaces and reality would be a colourful display of see-through objects and materials. But right now my view is blocked by the surfaces of things; my eyes create a reality that is defined by its very specific parameters, nothing more and nothing less. Not so much a limitation as it is (merely) a specific quality. Different beings have different receptors, different brains, causing different interpretations, different understandings, different realities.

What I see is a specific reality, my reality, and most probably we can see the same things with our eyes, but we don't. Our hardware is different, our filters are different, our interpretations, aware and unaware, are different. We are a projection of our different selves.

And then there was, the word

I think the power of the word relates to "Basic" programming, the first steps towards creating the virtual world/reality. There is another world beyond words, before words, after words, beneath words, around words, within words.

The meaning of words, the meaning of sentences, the

function of words, the function of sentences, their interpretation, their misinterpretation, their abuse.

When words do not capture the spirit of the thought, when the thought is beyond the words, when the thought is beyond words.

When the law is wrong, for missing the point, or for abusing the function of words of law. When the abuse of words is legal, because we allowed it to become legal.

When we gave the wrong people the power of words.

When the wrong people aspired to the power of words.

When the people believed the power of words.

When the people did not understand the power of words.

When the people did not feel the power of words.

When the people did not see the power of words.

When the people did not see.

When the people did not feel.

When the people did not understand.

When there was no meaning.

When the word, was just a word.

When the word, was not even a word.

The reality without this Existence

I imagine a reality without this Existence. A reality that is not a void, a reality that is nothing. A reality that is nowhere, because there is nowhere to be.

Then why are we here? To have more than other people?

Growth, the failure of Humanity.

Why does it always have to be "more"? How come we've become so accustomed to the idea, actually an illusion, that we need economic growth, or even more economic growth? How come we lost track of growing as humanity, as becoming more humane?

With structures of inequality built into our society, with governments that represent markets rather than human populations, a form of dehumanisation has grown into our understanding of what growth means for our societies. Inequality, with regards to financial or economical inequality, spreads into all aspects of life, it's like a cancer that justifies destroying, killing or eating everything new it can lay its tentacles on, as a form of self-preservation. This rather abstract view comes to life when you see it as an actual cancer, with Earth as the organism, and life on its surface as either benevolent or malevolent.

Growth as a human being, or as humanity as a whole, will be beneficial to Earth, our Existence. Economical growth has no other function than to line the pockets of those who already control and ruin our Existence. There is no need for international markets when we all can create the attributes needed for a prosperous life. Prosperous, as in being more humane, being more one with Earth, being more oneself, instead of being more financially rich etc. Growth as defined by lesser beings does not imply a world of wisdom, a world of intellectual richness, a world even of sentimental richness, of caring, of Justice, of Love.

So why do we allow "lesser beings" to define what growth means for our societies?

What a beautiful world this could be

What words would describe the beautiful world we all seem to long for? Peaceful? Clean? Healthy? Prosperous? Adventurous? Colourful? Magical? Loving? Caring? Challenging?

We have everything to make this world like"Heaven on Earth" for everyone, and yet, it is not so.

The good, the bad, and the beautiful

What words would describe the general world we all seem to live in? Violent? Polluted? Unhealthy? Destructive? Numbing? Contrasting? Dull? Repetitive? Hateful? Selfish? Challenging?

The good thing: it's challenging. The bad thing: on a global scale we see the same patterns, changing our world in a downward spiral, while it could have been everything else.

Dear world leaders

Enough is enough. You have had your chance to change the course for the good of humanity, and you didn't. Instead, you made matters worse by giving yourselves immunity from prosecution for all the corruption that you've been involved with. You do not seem to understand, you do not seem to feel, that a truly beautiful world is a beautiful world shared, a beautiful world cared for, not just a world of materialistic luxury shared by a small circle of corruptible selfish beings, and I carefully choose these words by not saying "human beings", because I have serious doubts whether you are human beings, or if you are just acting as if you are human beings. You may have the looks, but that does not make you human. You may have the suits and ties that give an illusion of decency, but they do not make you decent.

Illusions, they're all illusions, criminal illusions, in a world that already is an illusion. Illusions upon illusions. After all, what is real? Is what I see real? Is what you see real? What you hear? What you feel? What you touch? Or what touches you? What actually is this world? What is this reality? Does it really exist? Does it matter?

In a reality that exists in a time that never had a beginning, and never will end, does it matter how many houses you own, how many ships or Ferraris you own or how large the yacht is you own, how much money you've hoarded, how much you can be part of the glitter in tabloid media, at the expensive of anyone or everything else?

Yes it matters, because it shows you do not understand what life, this existence is about. It shows how poor-minded you are, how narrow-minded, how simple-minded, how small-minded you are, how selfish you are, how cold you are, how little human you are. One of the purposes of this life, this existence is to grow, to evolve, to become more and better than you were, than we were. What good is a world of abundance when it is not shared, when its joy is limited to the space within the walls around it. That's not joy. Imagine a world where you can freely walk out your front door, and share any and all joy, and people are happy to share it with you. That is joy.

Dear world leaders, your task is to make this a truly joyous world, for all. In this corruptible system it does not work, it can not work. There is no Justice in a world that justifies wars for profit, builds prisons for profit, creates spy networks for profit, because all control eventually is for profit. Greed is not a healthy state of mind. Greed in fact is quite similar to a mental disorder, maybe even is a mental disorder, and yet the most greedy seek positions of power, of people control, not caring, not sharing.

Maybe you've read George Orwell's "1984", it seems to have become a handbook for corporate exploitation and control. We see it all around us. Everywhere the same patterns; violence, national debt, asset sales, inequality. Is that the world you want for us?

Enough is enough. Dear world leaders, your task is to end the violence, to end national debt, to end asset sales, to end inequality, and to promote education, an informed populace, caring people, sharing people, people who enjoy making this the "Heaven on Earth" this could be, for all.

I'd like you to imagine, visualise this situation: my freedom ends where it meets yours. At that point it is about respect and trust. It's not a boundary, it's more like a no man's land, an arena for free speech, a showground for different perspectives, a place to meet as equals. Freedom.

Raising children

So many people, so many ideas of how to raise children.

Two words: respect and discipline. Our youth lacks respect, and lacks discipline, is what I read and hear on a regular basis from other adults. Some parents believe that to fulfil a social requirement of being respectful and/or disciplined they have to raise their children in a certain way that makes them look like good parents.

Why respect, why discipline? Firstly, it's what they've been told by their parents, and by their teachers. It's a repetition that slowly has been fading into an illusion that none of them seem to understand, so it's easier to just keep repeating it, as it seems right, right? When you decide to have children, I think it is essential to understand that the decision to have children was made by the parents, and not by the child(ren). The responsibility for the quality of life of the children therefore lies with the parents.

If parents do not understand the meaning of the word "respect", or if they do not understand whether or not it is "discipline" that they're after, then how can they be sure to be good parents?

Raising children is not an easy thing; the worst thing, however, I think is raising your children in the way you think that makes you look like a good parent. OK, there is an even worse way, not being a parent at all for your children, but that is an entirely different issue. Most people I know, see or hear do not comprehend the meaning of the word "respect", but as such that meaning is discussed elsewhere in this book. The other word, "discipline", is a misconception of what people believe is what they're missing in their children's attitude or behaviour. Discipline, however, is a very limited word; to me it relates to an army, obeying orders, and to illustrate my issue with the word discipline, I'd like to add, a lack of emotion. Discipline, at best, could be control of emotions, but in everyday parental life I think it just relates to obeying orders. Self-discipline is obeying your own orders.

What I think that discipline lacks is what the word "focus" invokes. Focus also relates to "vision". Lack of vision relates to lack of focus, and as such what most people refer to as "discipline", but which lacks the depth of vision. When parents do not have a proper, mature vision, they can not give their children an understanding of what really matters, and without that understanding there can not be a focus. Vision and focus are connected, literally and figuratively. Discipline, however, is just a word that expresses how much control you have.

Father and son, I

Distance. Physical distance, mental distance, emotional distance, or is it proximity? Or connection?

The relationship I had with my father, when I was about 17, was one of growing competition. Not from my part, but from his part. As I grew up, however, more and more I started to see that the illusion I had of who my father was, was breaking down, and I started to see who he really was. More and more I started to see him as a control freak, a power freak, manipulative, misleading and mentally abusive.

There was always this one story he was proud of to tell. It was from the time he was selling used cars on public car markets, many, many years ago. He once had a car for sale of which the reverse gear was broken; in Dutch the word for reverse gear is "achteruit" as one word, but with the same pronunciation as the word for rear window; "achteruit" and "achterruit"... So he then told, he'd damage the rear window of that car (which would be a relatively small cost to repair compared to a gearbox) and inform a buyer about a broken "achterruit", so the illusion of honesty was created. I do not know whether or not that story was true, but it does illustrate well what kind of a person he was. He wanted to make the impression of being an honest person, within the boundaries of the law as he saw it. But he did not care about the truth as long as he made a profit.

When I grew older, I wanted to buy my first car, as I needed one. As such I researched the market for available, sensible and affordable cars, and found a healthy-looking, orange-coloured Fiat 127 Sport, for fl.6,500. I can still see it standing outside at the car dealer, on the Varsseveldseweg in Doetinchem.

I asked my father if he would lend me the money, and he said no. Instead, he would sell me one of his own cars that he had for sale. It was a Ford Fiesta with a standard list price of about

Fl.15,000 that he enriched with various useless bells and whistles that he counted the full retail price for, all counting up to a price of more than fl.20,000.

He made up a document with all the legal bells and whistles he knew and copied from his last job as a car dealer and made me sign it and accept it as the only way I could get to a car. The story didn't end there. After about half a year I got into an accident and the wreck was sold, the monies collected from the insurance company, and a new car was bought. Again from my father, a naked Ford Fiesta, for fl.15,000. He had two of those for sale, though, and the other he sold shortly after to another car business, for fl.12,500.

This was the moment where all my doubts about my father became substantial and I no longer had any hope of ever finding the father I thought he could be.

The distance had become real. The distance had become like the Berlin Wall, complete with barbed wired perimeter, warning lights, German shepherd dogs and deadly bullets. If ever there could be a father behind it, I would never be able to reach him.

In later years, when I worked in the medical pharmaceutical industry with a specialisation in psychiatry, I kindly suggested to my father to have a talk with a therapist. Many years later I heard he had seen a therapist a few times, in secret, but never to the point it became a therapy. I knew some of his horrible youth, and hoped he had learnt from it, as to do things differently, better. He had chosen not to.

In a way I am thankful to my father, because he became

everything I did not want to be, which made it easier to see and understand who or what I wanted to be, as a person, as a husband, as a father. When he died, in 2004, I went to his funeral with my wife and son, and the best, the kindest I could think of was wishing him a great journey, wherever he would go.

Father and son, II

From the moment I became a father, in 1998, I was well aware that my life had changed in a substantial way. No longer was I only responsible for my own adult life, or to take good care of my wife and our life together, but from that moment on I was responsible for the future life of the child we brought into this world.

I imagined if he could be really happy in a world where he could have (almost) anything he wanted, and would be surrounded, and confronted, by a world that would consist of people who could not, who would be hurting, hungry, miserable, unhappy. I imagined that the only way I could make him truly happy was to make the world happy. And then 2008 happened, I had a close encounter with "something" that was not from this world, or from within these dimensions, and I knew that Life and Existence were not what I had been told throughout my life. Again, I knew I had to learn to understand this, not just for myself, but especially for our son.

When I look at the relationship I have with my son I see it would have been impossible to have anything like that with my own father, not even remotely, which makes me happy, sad and proud, all at the same time.

It's not easy growing up for a son, not when you had a father like I had, but also with a father like I am, I'm very aware of that. But, I treasure the distance, or rather the lack thereof, I see and feel between me and my son, and I know he sees and feels the same. And even if he would not, it would not change one bit for me, which is the one thing I've always made him aware of, "No matter what you do, or don't do, I will always love you and I will always be there for you".

We have a little black book that we used to write about the little lessons of life we had discussed. Little reminders, little dots in time, that would connect to a greater whole, somehow even as the structure of this book.

The Fermi paradox

The question Enrico Fermi asked, whether or not there is alien life out there, and if so, where the hell are they, is to me not a paradox at all. Simply put they are here, but we do not see them, or do not see them as such. What if we are blind? Not blind to the point that we see nothing, but blind to the point that there is more to see then we can see. Here I would refer to different levels of dimensions, but also different forms, or even non-forms of dimensions. My 2008 close encounter opened up my mind to what Donald Rumsfeld once called "the known-knowns, the known-unknowns, the unknown-knowns", but also the unknown-unknowns. Things that are way beyond our imagination (let alone understanding) because our hardware is not good enough to process the thought. It relates to the moment when I started to accept the idea that time never had a beginning, and therefore that Existence never had a beginning, and from this realisation, that anything that could happen, someday, somewhere will happen. Just give it enough time, and in infinite time, there is enough time.

So, the Fermi paradox. I have seen alien life, so for me there is no paradox, and as such it does not matter where it came from, or in what form. From studying history it seems they have been around for quite a while already. In a few old paintings, for instance from a Nuremberg event in 1561 that was described as a battle in the sky between objects of various shapes, of which some were described as orbs, we can see that the phenomenon is not unknown, and hardly new. I imagine that, once we've come to terms with their existence, integrated them into our existence, that there will be new forms, shapes, appearances, that we'll have to come to terms with before accepting them into our realities. Reality is more than what we think it is, and way more than we currently can see it is.

Apart from realities beyond our grasp, there still is a possibility that we're the only ones in the Universe, with the orbs being a lifeform that belongs to Earth, or near Earth. If there are no other forms of life out there, then why would the orbs travel out there? Or is it that the orbs came from elsewhere, to Earth, because they were attracted to our lifeforms? Are the orbs extra-terrestrial? Or extra-dimensional?

Because there had been no active communication with the

orb in my close encounter I can not answer such questions. I can make guesses, educated guesses, but that's about it. And I can influence, inspire others to change their views, their understandings, enrich their understanding as to enrich each others lives with better understandings. Communication is key, just as I see the simple appearance of the orb as communication. By simply showing itself, showing that existence is more.

Existence as being the ultimate form of being, layered, structured, in ways no man can experience in the dimensions we are in now, to me is compartmentalised in (at least) 5D where Earth actually is what religious people refer to as Heaven or Paradise. The confrontation with the Orb made clear that, as humans, in the Earthly conditions, we can have experiences that we can not have anywhere else. Experiences as an adventure, experiences to learn from, to learn lessons that can not be learned anywhere else in the Universe. Experiences also to enjoy, in multiple ways, with multiple senses, under multiple conditions, isn't this what "Heaven" would seem like? Isn't being, just being in Heaven?

Isn't this showing how we are allowing a few selfish, cold-hearted, warmongering assholes to ruin our Existence in Heaven?

Can there be a life after money?

Imagine a world without money, not even as a form of monetised bartering. A world that exists because people make it work for each other. A world where the highest goal is not collecting as much money as you can so you can buy (corrupt) people for selfish purposes, but a world where you are forced to look at things differently. When money is not the goal anymore, then what is?

We'd have to find the purpose of our Existence again. We'd have to start talking about what really matters again, we'll have to find our way again. We'd have to move forward, because there is no other way.

I think the first step would be to step away from this system where hoarding money has become like a religious virtue, as if more money represents a better human being, while in essence the actual opposite is true. Hoarding millions, or even billions of dollars, is taking those amounts out of the circulation, out of the system, meaning there is less for billions of people to share.

For the purpose of monetised bartering all money should be flowing freely in the financial system, like blood enables the transport to and from anything to anywhere in our bodies. By taking blood out, the circulation becomes less effective, even at the risk of causing damage. The human body can repair itself by making more blood, but when it is poorly nurtured even that becomes less effective, like a downward spiral.

The way it is going now humanity is following that same path, from multiple points of view. There is the corrupt, multinational organised criminal cancer that is growing all over the world, eating, destroying and infecting anything and everything (including governments) that comes in its path, and at the same time we see the blood that is continuously being taken out of the circulation. This is the picture of a dying living being. This is a picture of a living being that is being taken over by a cancer, a cancer that does not care, a cancer that can not care, because it is inherently connected to how, to what the cancer is. But we know better, or do we?

Towards a conclusion

When you are, have become, fully aware of the 4 dimensions, the 3 spatial dimensions + time, then you can glimpse through the hole in the barrier, upwards towards the 5th dimensional group.

Just because most humans can not see it, does that mean it does not exist? (As absence of evidence still is not evidence of absence.)

Before the invention of the microscope, did bacteria and viruses exist? Or did they come into existence after the invention of the microscope?

We are waiting for the invention of the multiversal scope; however, it may not be viewed/experienced from within our world, our 4 dimensions, but a lower-dimensional presentation/projection in(to) our reality may be possible?

It starts with a question, followed by a theory and research. What will follow may go beyond your wildest imagination. What if the space around us is filled with "life", but we can not see it, because our "hardware", our "programs" do not provide the means to see it, and our limited understanding of what "life" is blocks our view?

Awareness has a span, a "mass", a "density", in multiple directions/dimensions. The here and now is different for every individual. In a 2D world the awareness of that 2D world must be in a cloud, a higher reality.

Different humans have different speeds, different internal clocks, that though they can synchronise them with external clocks, will make them live in different worlds that only seem the same to the unaware eye.

Maybe, what we call the 3-dimensional world actually is just the 1st dimension, with or without the 4th dimension, time, where time just is the catalyst into other dimensions. The 1st dimension is our current reality, and most people believe we all just see the same, though the reality is, we all believe differently. When people choose to believe anything, any "reality", they choose to accept as truth something that is not necessarily true, they choose to believe it is true. To me this is a choice to put blindfolds on, heavily tinted shades, that filter out realities that conflict with one's beliefs. Reality, however, is so beautiful that it should not be filtered out. Any filter will block out an entire dynamic range, not just the little part you don't want to see. With more beauty, though, also comes more ugliness. That's the deeper reality, the bigger reality, the reality that grows. The reality that grows into deeper understanding, deeper awareness, a different world.

Finishing this journey we arrive again at the final question, the question where every research will end, it's the question that one can not escape from, which is why organised religions were invented, to avoid asking that question.

Time never had a beginning; whatever time is, whatever time could be, it never had a beginning. No matter what dimensions, no matter what direction, no matter how big or how small, no matter what you can understand or not, time never had a beginning. And because time never had a beginning, Existence also never had a beginning; again, no matter what form, shape or dimensions, Existence never had a beginning. This means that there always had been endless time to think about this, there always had been endless opportunities to think about this, and what to do with it.

Even in a trial-and-error model, endless time gives opportunities to let anything happen, anything imaginable, and unimaginable. The conclusion from that must be that the final question has been asked before, and has been asked numerous times. Therefore organised religions were a solution to prevent beings, in our case human beings, from questioning the purpose of their daily lives.

The purpose of Life is to give meaning to Existence. Without Life Existence has no meaning, it just is. No plants growing, no insects crawling, no birds flying, no fish swimming, no humans thinking, not even alien life hovering. Just rocks, mountains, water, wind, clouds, sand, dust. Just being, without life, without thought, without emotion, without Love. Life gives meaning to Existence, the purpose of Life is to give meaning to Existence.

Then what about Existence itself?

What is the purpose of Existence?

What is the point?

Existence has no purpose, Existence merely is its own purpose. Existence as such is a loop, we're trapped in a loop, we're going in circles. But then, learning from it, the circle becomes a spiral, in whatever direction. And still, Existence has no purpose, it has no goal, no matter what direction it is going. There is no reward to Existence, and even if there was, what purpose would it have? A self-gratification?

We can learn, we can evolve, we can become better beings, we can become different beings, we can grow into other dimensions. But to what purpose? We can learn to understand ever more about this Existence, about this dimension, about other dimensions, but in the end it serves no purpose.

The fact that in this endless Universe, or Multiverse (whatever that may be), there may be another person just like me, sitting, thinking, doing the exact same thing that I'm doing, scares me. The absurdness of an Existence that has no purpose but, at best, being it's own purpose, and then replicated in a moment and place of unknown distance (time, place, dimension) to me feels like something that is unacceptable. What is the point of it?

I think it was a little after the birth of my son that my thinking and understanding towards the Essence of this Existence became denser and denser, and for that the Essence became more compact, more focused, more isolated, more to the point, more essential. It was then that my wife said "one day you'll take a piece of paper and a pencil, and you'll place a dot on that piece of paper, exactly on the right spot. And that will say it all, that will be the point of it all".

The Essence has a tendency to be both complex and simple at the same time, depending on the point of view, the perspective.

In fact you can choose to see the Essence in its simplicity or in its complexity, and the path that I was following was to find the Essence in its simplicity, in fact in its most essential beauty. Beauty is complete, honest, true, it is at peace, in balance. Therefore, the final question should be one that exposes beauty, the essential beauty of our existence. So, does it?

In Essence, my search started after the close encounter in 2008, with the hovering plasma light orb, with its gentle light structure. It showed me that Life, Existence, are not what we've been told over many generations, it showed me that endless time provides for endless opportunities to use or abuse this Existence, while learning how to do that best, both good and bad. And what is good, or bad in the first place? Why wouldn't what we as human beings on Earth perceive as bad be good from a different point of view, from a different culture, from a different lifeform, from a different existence? Why wouldn't a different lifeform have learned, over millions of years of time, how to keep beings, like human beings, for instance to make them dig up gold, and then collect it at some point in time? What is the point of it being given an illusion of value, expressed in another illusion we call money? What's the point of all this, if it leaves the majority of human beings suffering under the pressure of not having enough money, while a small percentage just live a life of waste at the cost of the rest, at the cost of all the rest, including health, nature, the oceans, all of it?

What is the point?

I mean, even if there is a Heaven as all organised religions suggest, whatever a Heaven may be, what is the point of an endless

Heaven? Then what is the point of having life on Earth at all? Why not hang out with the virgins from the beginning, if there was a beginning at all? For any loving God, for any loving father, he'd only want the best for you, he'd want you to be happy, to be loved. To give, and to accept, to share, to care, all in the name of Love and not just love that is mostly lust, greed or want.

I would imagine this life on Earth as a place to learn, or even as a holiday to learn. Things that one can only learn on Earth, because of its specific qualities of Existence. Here you can learn to understand what Love is in a far different way than one could learn it on the Moon, or the Sun, or Jupiter if you wish. Is this life on Earth of such quality, so different from other dimensions, that "beings" would choose to experience this part, this dimension, of Existence, of their Existence, as a form of learning holiday? And then, after that, Heaven, endless Heaven? Or a different dimension, a new level of experience, with bonus points for achievements?

Why would we call our God a God of Love, when the experience always ends in pain? Is the purpose of this experience more than just this life, is it part of a bigger plan? But then again, what's the point of that? What's the point of learning to understand what Love is, and seeing that what organised religions tell people is not Love, but control, people control, whereas learning Love would be, should be, about teaching what Freedom is, what Respect is, what Trust is, and how they form the basis on which Love can grow?

Are we there yet?

In an enclosed environment energy stays at an equilibrium. About 20% of energy consumption happens in our brain, our mind. Where does the brain become the mind? Are my thoughts in my head, or are they larger than that?

Are my thoughts energy? If yes, can they change into mass? In other words, can they create, bring into existence, materialise into a new touchable object?

Or do my thoughts happen in a different plane, a different dimension, a different reality than my physical being? Would that explain what dreams are, partly or in whole?

Are we creating this world into existence? Or can we change the course of history by collective aim of thought? Is the difference between us and "God" a switched-off capacity to create, materialise thought? Then, where is the switch? In what form or dimension does it exist? What are the thoughtmakers? We are the thoughtmakers, but what are thoughts? How are thoughts different from the bunches of atoms and molecules flying around in space in the form of what we call humans? Or are they not flying around and is it just our collective thought, a collective "dream state", in a form, a dimension, that we call "Existence", or "Reality", or "The here and now". What is awareness?

From the point of view of strategic global manipulations, as the world is functioning now, I see this world as a 4D game of chess, where the 4th dimension would be Time. And for the sake of keeping things simple we'll use Time as the linear reality we're existing in now together, on this Earth.

In 4D our Earth is a structure of lines, networks, connecting similar entities with each other in one layer, and other entities in other layers. Similarly to beings living in a 2D world, the different layers are separated, to a certain extent. Many people are only aware of the layer they exist in, it's their reality. Their reality may have some extensions into nearby layers, and mostly that's it. To be fully aware of the vastness of the Greater Reality, we'd probably need a different set of brains. When I was a boy I wanted to know everything, and soon learned I can not know everything. How can I know what is happening in all other places around the world? So I decided that that's not it. I needed to simplify, I needed to put it in structures that catch the Essence(s) of it all. I thought "When I understand the Essences, I can project that on similar issues, without actually knowing them, and still understand them".

In 1997, for a multimedia class at the California College of (the) Arts (and Crafts, as it was called then), I made a 4D structure for a multimedia game, unaware of it actually being 4D. My goal was to find a different way of functioning for video games, as I saw always two choices that would form the path to follow. So instead of two choices, I made a triangular pyramid that would always give me three choices, upon three choices, upon three choices, as the triangular pyramids formed the structure, which would give "endless" different paths, in any direction, and fast, through a game with minimum structure and maximum strength.

This was to form the same structure of how I would see the world in 4D, and later, as 5D. Different layers, with highways through them in all directions, connecting everything to everything. Well, everything that I thought essential to keep the structures visible, clear, understandable. A structure of everything, to help me understand the essence of everything, the essence of Existence.

If the Final question would be, "What is the purpose of Existence?", my initial answer used to be "There is none." But then, in a strange way, it seemed, that maybe Existence is its own purpose.

Well, I think we'll have to face it, both "Existence has no purpose", and "Existence is its own purpose" are true. Is it the ultimate duality? It's something I can live with, it adds to life's mysteries, it adds to life's wonder, its beauty, and ugliness. But then again, from a different perspective, from a different dimension, it may all just be part of the beauty of Existence itself.

In the meantime we'll have to make it worthwhile, see what can not be seen elsewhere, experience what can not be experienced elsewhere, live as can not be lived elsewhere, and learn what can not be learned elsewhere in the multiverse. Life on Earth offers unique qualities, unique limitations. Out of those limitations come unique opportunities to experience and to learn. They make Earth some kind of holiday resort compared to other places in space. They make life on Earth like a holiday from life in space or even from life in other dimensions. There is no other place in the multiverse where we can experience the beauty and the ugliness that can be experienced here on Earth. Is that what those five seconds were about? Or was it to show a different form of energy, or even a different form of reality? Or was it just to say hello? Five seconds may not seem like much, but they now mean the world to me, an endless world that is.

The End

FIVE SECONDS

Index of images:

18 Begijnhof, Amsterdam.

22 Ceramics V.O.C., "De Gouden Eeuw", Amsterdam museum.

27 Sarcophagus lid Djedhor 4th century BC, Louvre Museum, Paris.

31 Felix Meritis building, Amsterdam.

35, 36, 37 Views from top of Felix Meritis building.

38, 39, 40, 42 Felix Meritis building interior.

43 Ramses Shaffy, Dutch National Archives, The Hague.

44 View from top of Felix Meritis building.

45 Zuiderkerk, Amsterdam.

46, 47, 48 Impressions around the canals, Amsterdam.

49 Begijnhof, Amsterdam.

50, 51 Brandevoort, Helmond.

56 Roggestraat, Doesburg, view West.

57 Roggestraat, Doesburg, view East, De Waag.

62, 63 Buckingham Palace, London.

65 Room with a view of bureaucrats, London.

66, 68, 69 Trafalgar Square, London.

70, 71 Battersea Power Station, London.

72 Westminster Abbey, Leicester Square.

73 Buckingham Palace.

74, 75, 76, 77 Bureaucratic signs, London.

79 Interior Chateau Versailles.

80, 81 Gare du Nord, Paris.

82, 83 Eiffel Tower, Paris, view North.

84 Gare Javel, Paris, Versailles.

85 Trocadero, Paris.

86 Dagobert 1er, Versailles.

87 Chateau Versailles.

94 Hovering light orb, Tamahere, New Zealand.

95, 96, 97 Light orb.

110 Buckingham Palace, London.

111 The Diana Princess of Wales Memorial Walk, London.

117 Design for a "500 year house" in the Hakarimata, John van Zeist.

121 Rietveld Lyceum, Doetinchem.

126, 127 Design for a patent construction lightweight house, John van Zeist.

143 The sun climbing over the Kaimai Range, New Zealand.

207 White Island, New Zealand.

262 Notre Dame, Paris.

265 Baseball wisdom.

273 My mother, about 1935, 2nd from the left, Friesland, the Netherlands.

All pictures copyright John van Zeist, except page 43, Ramses Shaffy, from the Dutch National Archives in The Hague, the Netherlands.

References:

"Moordenaars van Jan de Witt", Ronald Prud'Homme

Rijksmuseum

Amsterdam museum

http://www.denhaag.nl/en/residents/to/History-of-the-Dutch-Royal-Family.htm

"De Republiek", "Politeia", Plato

"The Art of War", Sun Tzu

"The saying of Wu Tzu"

"To Kill a Mockingbird", Harper Lee

"Animal Farm", George Orwell

"Im Westen Nichts Neues", Erich Maria Remarque

"The Passionless People Revisited", Gordon McLauchlan

Heraclitus, fragments of. (no. 38)

O.A.C.C.I.S., thesis 1997, John van Zeist

"Corruption and Market in Contemporary China", Yan Sun

"The Quants", Scott Patterson

FIVE SECONDS

www.ingramcontent.com/pod-product-compliance
Lightning Source LLC
Chambersburg PA
CBHW052013290426
44112CB00014B/2223